SpringerBriefs in Business

More information about this series at http://www.springer.com/series/8860

Pietro Gottardo • Anna Maria Moisello

Capital Structure, Earnings Management, and Risk of Financial Distress

A Comparative Analysis of Family and Non-family Firms

Springer

Pietro Gottardo
Department of Economics
and Management
University of Pavia
Pavia, Italy

Anna Maria Moisello
Department of Economics
and Management
University of Pavia
Pavia, Italy

ISSN 2191-5482 ISSN 2191-5490 (electronic)
SpringerBriefs in Business
ISBN 978-3-030-00343-2 ISBN 978-3-030-00344-9 (eBook)
https://doi.org/10.1007/978-3-030-00344-9

Library of Congress Control Number: 2018952487

This Springer imprint is published by the registered company Springer Nature Switzerland AG
The registered company address is: Gewerbestrasse 11, 6330 Cham, Switzerland

Contents

1 Introduction . . . 1
1.1 Introduction . . . 1
1.2 Background . . . 3
1.3 Target Audience . . . 5
1.4 Summary and Chapter Breakdown . . . 7
References . . . 8

2 Family Control and Capital Structure Choices . . . 13
2.1 Introduction . . . 13
2.2 Background and Hypothesis Development . . . 15
2.3 Research Methodology . . . 21
2.3.1 Data . . . 21
2.3.2 Variables . . . 23
2.3.3 Methods . . . 24
2.4 Results and Robustness Checks . . . 24
2.5 Discussion . . . 31
2.6 Contributions and Implications . . . 33
2.6.1 Limitations and Future Research . . . 34
References . . . 35

3 Family Influence, Leverage and Probability of Financial Distress . . . 41
3.1 Introduction . . . 41
3.2 Theoretical Background and Hypothesis Development . . . 42
3.2.1 Sew and Risk Taking . . . 43
3.2.2 Hypothesis Development . . . 45
3.3 Data and Methods . . . 46
3.4 Results and Discussion . . . 48
3.5 Implications and Challenges . . . 51
References . . . 52

4 Equity and Bond Issues and Earnings Management Practices 57
4.1 Introduction 57
4.2 Background and Hypothesis Development 58
4.2.1 Earnings Management, Equity and Debt 58
4.2.2 Earnings Management in Family Firms 60
4.2.3 Hypothesis Development 61
4.3 Methodology 63
4.4 Results 64
4.5 Discussion 67
4.6 Implications, Limitations and Suggestions for Further Studies 69
References 70

5 Earnings Management, Issues and Firm Market Value 75
5.1 Introduction 75
5.2 Literary Review and Hypothesis Development 77
5.2.1 Earnings Management and Market Performance 77
5.2.2 Family Firm's Performance 78
5.2.3 Socioemotional Wealth, Earnings Management and Market Value 79
5.3 Methodology 81
5.3.1 Data 81
5.3.2 Variables 82
5.3.3 Methods 83
5.4 Results 84
5.5 Discussion 86
5.6 Implications, Limitations and Avenues for Future Research 88
References 88

6 Conclusions 93
6.1 Introduction 93
6.2 Research Overview 94
6.3 Future Research 96
References 98

Chapter 1
Introduction

Abstract Family businesses are a leading organizational form in economies all over the world. There is a growing interest around family firms' financial behavior, in terms of financing and investment choices, performance, and disclosure, as a number of questions are still open. In this chapter we present the literature background and our research questions. Theoretical and methodological choices, structure of the book and target audience are illustrated as well.

1.1 Introduction

According to the Family Firms' Institute, family companies account for two-thirds of all companies around the world, they produce more than 70% of global GDP annually and they contribute to job creation all over the world providing 50–80% of the whole employment.[1] Literature provides evidence of the peculiarity of their behavior compared to non-family firms and of the heterogeneity among family companies themselves. Research suggests that family firms are led not only by financial but also by non-financial goals and recent literature argues that family businesses' reference point is the preservation of socioemotional wealth (Gómez-Mejía et al. 2007; Cruz et al. 2012; Leitterstorf and Rau 2014). The concept of socioemotional wealth (SEW) refers to "the stock of affect-related value that a family derives from its controlling position in a particular firm" (Berrone et al. 2012, p. 259). SEW is characterized by several dimensions: family control and influence on the business, identification of family members with the firm, binding social ties, emotional attachment of family members and renewal of family bonds to the firm through dynastic succession (Berrone et al. 2012). The relevance they assume make family different from non-family firms and determine family businesses' heterogeneity (Gómez-Mejía et al. 2011; Vandekerkhof et al. 2015). The socioemotional wealth framework is raising a great deal of interest among scholars,

[1]http://www.ffi.org/?page = GlobalDataPoints. Last accessed 18th April 2018.

P. Gottardo, A. M. Moisello, *Capital Structure, Earnings Management, and Risk of Financial Distress*, SpringerBriefs in Business,
https://doi.org/10.1007/978-3-030-00344-9_1

as demonstrated by the growing body of literature related to SEW. Research has provided empirical evidence that SEW preservation affects a firm's risk-taking behavior (Gómez-Mejía et al. 2007), capital structure choices (Gottardo and Moisello 2014), investments (Gómez-Mejía et al. 2014a), acquisitions (Gómez-Mejía et al. 2018), IPO underpricing (Leitterstorf and Rau 2014; Kotlar et al. 2018), delisting decisions (Boers et al. 2017), earnings management practices (Stockmans et al. 2010; Pazzaglia et al. 2013; Martin et al. 2016), and financial and non-financial disclosure (Gómez-Mejía et al. 2014b; Gavana et al. 2017). Literature has addressed specific topics related to a firm's financial behavior, in terms of financing and investment choices, performance, and disclosure. Given the relevance of these issues for investors and a broad range of a company's stakeholders, there is a need for a comprehensive analysis of these topics in order to learn more about the relations between them. We know that family firms are concerned with preserving the emotional value that the owning family experiences by exerting its control and influence over the firm, and for this reason, they are less prone than non-family firms to open their equity (Gottardo and Moisello 2014). The strong identification between the family and the company enhances family business' reputational concerns, affecting its disclosure and resulting in higher earnings' quality than their non-family counterparts. From these starting points emerge several research questions: How do different forms of family influence affect a firm's leverage? Does leverage affect family firms' capability to prevent financial distress? How does family influence affect earnings quality in cases of bond and equity issues? Does earnings quality affect market performance in family firms?

We address these research questions by drawing on the socioemotional wealth framework integrated with financial theories, i.e. Pecking Order Theory, Trade off Theory and Agency Theory. From the methodological point of view, we analyze longitudinal samples of Italian family and non-family non-financial firms. The Italian setting is of particular interest for different reasons. The first is that, in Italy, 94% GDP is produced by family businesses and 93% of the private sector is made up of family companies.[2] The second is that Italy is a peculiar setting for analyzing the effect of the SEW dimension related to family control and influence because families are particularly committed to maintaining control of the firm: as reported by Franks et al. (2011), for family companies starting from a 100% stake, diluting ownership below 25% of voting rights would take, on average, 20 years in the U.K., 30 years in Germany, 35 in France and more than 90 years in Italy. The third is that Italy relies on a bank-based economy and a large majority of studies related to this topic analyze market-based economies. The remainder of the chapter is structured as follows: the next section presents the theoretical background. The third section identifies the target audience. In the fourth section we present the summary and the chapter breakdown.

[2]http://www.ffi.org/?page = GlobalDataPoints. Last accessed 18th April 2018.

1.2 Background

Defining the family firms is a very challenging issue for family business researchers (Handler 1989) and literature suggests various definitions which may rely on ownership, family involvement in management, generational transfer and family business culture (Astrachan et al. 2002). Shanker and Astrachan (1996) classify family business definitions, provided by literature, into “wide”, “intermediate” and “restrictive”. According to the wide definition a firm is a family business whether its main strategies are controlled by a family even though they are not formulated by family members. In this vein, Anderson et al. (2003) use an ownership-based definition, as well as more recent literature (Miralles-Marcelo et al. 2014). Anderson and Reeb (2003a) define a firm a family business when the founding family holds an ownership stake in the company and/or family members sit on the board. Intermediate definition requires that family members, founders or descendants, control a firm’s equity and are directly involved in management, but not exclusively. As a matter of fact, scholars differently describe family direct involvement. McConaughy et al. (2001) assume that a family firm is led by a member of the controlling family. Fahlenbrach (2009) individuates a family company when the CEO is the founder or co-founder of the firm, Gómez-Mejía et al. (2007) define a family business as one that is controlled and managed by the founding family. The restrictive definition highlights the role of generational transfer and requires that several generations of a family exert ownership control and engage in a company’s management. Accordingly, Chrisman et al. (2004) assess family involvement in the business in terms of ownership, management and the trans-generational intent to maintain the leadership of business within the family. In particular, Colli et al. (2003) call a family business a company characterized by, at least, two generation of family control, led by a family CEO, and a minimum of 5% of voting rights held by the family. Despite the variety of definitions assumed by literature, scholars agree that a family firm is one whose business is much influenced by an owning family and its objectives (Gómez-Mejía et al. 2011).

According to the SEW perspective, based on the Behavioral Agency Model (Wiseman and Gómez-Mejía 1998; Gómez-Mejía et al. 2000), family businesses act in order to increase or preserve the stock of emotional value invested in the firm (Gómez-Mejía et al. 2007). The SEW construct encompasses different non-financial aspects of the business that meet the family’s affective needs (Gómez-Mejía et al. 2010). Literature identifies five dimensions as the main non-financial utilities: family control and influence on the business, identification of family members with the firm, binding social ties, emotional attachment of family members and renewal of family bonds to the firm through dynastic succession (Berrone et al. 2012). Tight linkage binds family members to the firm, so they derive a strong emotional return from family influence and control over the business. The extent of family control through ownership on the one hand affects the importance of the pursuit of socioemotional wealth and, on the other, the power and sense of legitimacy by which the family supports decisions to enhance the non-financial returns of the business (Zellweger et al. 2011). Families experience strong emotional ties and a strong sense of identification with the firm, which is perceived as an extension of the family itself (Berrone et al. 2012). Family firms protect this sense of identification and they behave not only in order to preserve the family's control, but they are also reluctant to open their equity to non-family investors (Romano et al. 2000). Through the business, a family develops important bonds with employees, which become part of a sort of extended family, as well as with suppliers and with the community in which the company operates. These social links meet a family's affective needs for belonging and provide a sense of legacy, giving family members relevant emotional returns (Berrone et al. 2012; Gómez-Mejía et al. 2011; Astrachan and Jaskiewicz 2008). Families get affective returns in terms of present as well as future benefits of control (Zellweger et al. 2011) because a firm is a long-term investment that should be passed to future generations in order to renew the family bonds to the business and to meet the emotional need to perpetuate the family dynasty (Berrone et al. 2010; Berrone et al. 2012). Gómez-Mejía et al. (2007, p. 108) say that preserving SEW "represents a key goal in and of itself. In turn, achieving this goal requires continued family control of the firm", and, for this reason, families are more prone to preserve a firm's control than non-family owners.

The preservation of socioemotional wealth is the reference point in family firms' risk-taking decisions and makes family businesses risk averse and risk willing at the same time (Gómez-Mejía et al. 2007). They are prone to put at risk financial performance in order to preserve family control as they think that they can manage this type of hazard, but when performance is below target they do not try to increase it by investing in high variance ventures (Gómez-Mejía et al. 2007) as putting the survival of the company at risk jeopardizes the financial and non-financial benefits that the family derives from it.

There is evidence that the way the family exerts its control influences a firm's attitudes towards risk as family companies are less risk averse when they are managed by a non-family CEO (Huybrechts et al. 2013). Moreover, a family's form of involvement in the business affects the company's diversification choices (Muñoz-Bullon et al. 2017). We know that family ownership also affects a company's risk-taking behavior in terms of capital structure and debt level and that firms are prone to assume leverage risk to avoid family control dilution (Gottardo and Moisello 2014; Bacci et al. 2017). Given the evidence found on the above-cited forms of risk, it is of interest to analyze how different forms of family involvement may influence a firm's leverage. It is also of interest to verify how leverage risk meets a family firm's expectations, in terms of long-term survival, and to analyze its effect on a company's probability of running into financial distress.

Some studies have analyzed the relation between a firm's financing decisions and its earnings quality. Literature supplies empirical evidence of earnings management (EM) activities around IPOs and SEOs and debt issues, providing mixed results in relation to investors' perceptions of EM (Rangan 1998; Teoh et al. 1998; Shivakumar 2000; Cohen and Zarowin 2010; Roosenboom et al. 2003; Fan 2007; Liu et al. 2010; Ghosh and Moon 2010). No study has yet analyzed the effect of family control and influence on earnings management activities around equity and debt emissions or examined investors' response to reported earnings manipulations in terms of a firm's market valuation.

We know that family firms provide more transparent financial information than non-family companies (Martin et al. 2016), although they may manage reported earnings downward to decrease dividends and/or taxation so as to increase self-financing and avoid resorting to external investors (Achleitner et al. 2014). Nevertheless, family businesses may upward report earnings in order to prevent board member appointments by lenders or covenant restrictions, or a reduction in terms of debt financing opportunities (Prencipe et al. 2008; Stockmans et al. 2010). Overall, there is evidence that family firms are less prone to resort to earnings management practices than non-family firms, although their earnings quality may be affected by the need to preserve the current sources of financing, but there is no evidence on their reporting behavior in cases of bond and equity issues.

Research has widely explored the effect of different forms of family influence on a firm's operating performance and market value. There is evidence that family firms present a higher performance than their non-family counterparts (Anderson and Reeb 2003b; Vieira 2014). Findings suggest that family involvement in management positively affects a firm's performance in later generational stages, when financial objectives become more salient than non-financial returns (Sciascia et al. 2014), whilst a U-shaped relationship links the number of family advisors and family firm performance (Naldi et al. 2015) as well as the percentage of family members on the top management team and a company's financial performance (Chirico and Bau 2014). There is also evidence of a positive effect of family control on a company's operating performance and value, when the founder is alive and is still exerting his/her influence (Barontini and Caprio 2006; Villalonga and Amit 2006), whilst the owner's heirs may get worse performance than professional CEOs in older firms (Morck et al. 1988; Bennedsen and Nielsen 2010).

Literature suggests that EM practices may be value-relevant as reported by studies that analyze earnings management practices around emissions (Rangan 1998; Teoh et al. 1998), highlighting that the stock market efficiently provides an answer to earnings manipulations (Shivakumar 2000). To the best of our knowledge, no studies have focused on family firms. We have no evidence whether earnings management practices affect family firms' market value, in case of issues, in the presence of different forms of family involvement in the business.

1.3 Target Audience

The research questions addressed by this book meet the interest of a wide and diversified audience. This work is primarily conceived for researchers and scholars of family firms as it analyzes questions that engage the debate in this field of study and some topics that have not been previously addressed when focusing on family firms. Researchers point out that finance is an area of growing interest in the field of family businesses (Benavides-Velasco et al. 2013; Voordeckers et al. 2014). Family firms' capital structure choices are a timely issue: very recent literature has studied family firms' leverage in the pre- and post-crisis period (Migliori et al. 2018), therefore this book contributes to the debate by reporting findings on the effect of leverage on family and non-family firms' probability to run into financial distress, controlling for the crisis period.

This work is also of interest for accounting and finance researchers as it analyzes a relevant topic related to accounting choices, i.e. earnings management in family firms and the relation with financing choices and a firm's market performance. Family firms' accounting choices is a relatively-explored theme that is increasingly attracting the interest of family business scholars. The recent book by Ferramosca and Ghio (2018) on family firms' accounting choices points out the great interest and need for research on these topics and our empirical study complements their theoretical work well. Moreover, for each issue analyzed, the book provides suggestions and avenues for further research.

Family firms' ubiquity in economies across the world attracts great attention by academics from the research and teaching point of view. A growing number of universities are introducing family business courses into their curricula (Ferramosca and Ghio 2018), not only in North America but across Europe. Italian universities are also investing in international experts to manage these courses and in the creation of centers for family business management, as recently occurred at the University of Bolzano. Therefore, this book may interest teachers as well as students engaged in their final dissertation as it provides useful material and data for discussion.

The book supplies significant information for investors as it provides findings on family and non-family firms' earnings management practices, which may result in severe negative consequences for this type of stakeholder, in cases of equity and bond emissions. Moreover, it presents data on the effect of some governance and financial characteristics on a firm's likelihood to encounter financial distress.

The reported results are of interest for policy makers and regulators because of the effect that family firms' financing and accounting choices may have on the capital market, the former in terms of the number of listed firms and capitalization, the latter in terms of information asymmetries detrimental to its efficiency. European policies take into account financing capabilities as a major concern for family companies (European Commission 2015). Moreover, family businesses, as suggested by the Family Firms Institute,[3] create over five million jobs in Europe (40–50% of all employment), they are more prone to supply stable employment as they are less likely to lay off staff and to hire when facing the possibility of an economic downturn. They engage in charitably activities and support their respective communities. Their performance and long-term survival have relevant social implications. Therefore, information on the determinants of their probability of financial distress and market performance is of interest for the regulating activity. It is also relevant for

[3]http://www.ffi.org/?page = GlobalDataPoints. Last accessed 18th April 2018.

family firms as they can observe how the intention to preserve family control and influence may affect these crucial aspects for a company's long-term survival.

1.4 Summary and Chapter Breakdown

The book is articulated in six chapters:

Chapter 1 Introduction
Chapter 1 presents an overview of the book: the literature background, the aim of the book, the theoretical and methodological choices, the structure of the book and the target audience.

Chapter 2 Family Control and Capital Structure Choices
Chapter 2 analyzes the capital structure choices of family firms. It draws on the socioemotional wealth approach combined with capital structure theories, i.e. Pecking Order Theory (POT) and Trade Off Theory (TOT) in order to measure the impact of family control and influence on a firm's capital structure. Using a large sample of private and listed medium-large Italian firms over the period 2001–2010, it argues that the differences in leverage between family and non-family firms and among family businesses are affected by the family and control dimension of the socioemotional wealth. Family ownership and family involvement in management help explain family firms' behavior. The results indicate that the preservation of the family endowment in the business influences firms' attitude toward leverage. The presence of multiple family members on the board and in executive positions and a firm's first generational stage increase this effect, while ownership dispersion has a moderating effect. We conclude by highlighting the implications, limitations of this study as well as venues for further research.

Chapter 3 Family Influence, Leverage and Probability of Financial Distress
This Chapter analyzes leverage's effect on a company's likelihood of financial distress. In particular we analyze the effect of the ultimate controlling owner nature, that is family or non-family control, on a firm's likelihood to run into financial distress. We address this topic by using a large sample of Italian private family and non-family firms, and by drawing on the Socioemotional wealth framework. We also consider other risk measures in addition to leverage, as well as, board and CEO characteristics, accounting variables and macroeconomic indicators.

All in all, our results show that family firms are less likely to incur financial distress than non-family firms. Leverage significantly increases the probability of financial distress for family and non-family firms, but a family's direct influence on the firm, by appointing a family CEO, has a significant moderating effect on this probability.

Chapter 4 Equity and Bond Issues and Earnings Management Practices
Chapter 4, drawing on Agency Theory integrated with socioemotional wealth, analyzes the effect of equity and bond issues on earnings management practices,

and compares family and non-family firms' earnings management behavior in case of emissions. In so doing, it analyzes a sample of 239 non-financial listed firms for the period 2007–2015. It provides evidence that, although family firms are less prone than their non-family counterparts to manage reported earnings, in cases of equity emissions, they significantly increase this practice. However, the effect is lower than for non-family businesses. Findings do not indicate a significant effect in cases of bond emissions. The results suggest that the presence of the founder has an opposite effect on family and non-family firms' earnings management practices: in family firms it significantly moderates this unethical behavior whilst and in the presence of equity emissions, this beneficial effect does not change. The chapter concludes by providing some considerations on the implications of our findings, limitations and further research developments.

Chapter 5 Earnings Management, Issues and Firm Market Value
Chapter 5 addresses the issue of accounting choices value relevance. We study the effect of earnings quality on a firm's market value by analyzing the sample we introduced in Chap. 4, drawing on Agency Theory integrated with the Socioemotional wealth perspective. In so doing we take into account equity and bond emissions and we control for the effect of non-financial voluntary disclosure quality, in order to supply a comprehensive picture of the effect of family companies' communication choices. Our findings suggest that these choices differently affect family and non-family firms' market value. In particular, on the one hand, we find that earnings management has a significant negative effect on non-family companies' market performance whilst it does not affect family firms' market value in a significant way. On the other hand, we provide empirical evidence of a significant positive relation between voluntary non-financial disclosure and market value for family businesses, but the relationship is not significant for non-family firms. The type of family influence on the business does not change these effects. We close the chapter by underlining the implications of our results, limitations as well as future challenges for research.

Chapter 6 Conclusion
Chapter 6 provides some final considerations, pointing out the contributions and implications of the present work for academics, managers, practitioners and policy makers. It also complements the suggestions for further research provided in the previous chapters from a broader perspective.

References

Achleitner, A. K., Günther, N., Kaserer, C., & Siciliano, G. (2014). Real earnings management and accrual-based earnings management in family firms. *European Accounting Review, 23*(3), 431–461.

Anderson, R. C., & Reeb, D. M. (2003a). Founding-family ownership, corporate diversification, and firm leverage. *The Journal of Law and Economics, 46*(2), 653–684.

Anderson, R. C., & Reeb, D. M. (2003b). Founding-family ownership and firm performance: Evidence from the S&P 500. *Journal of Finance, 58*(3), 1301–1328.

Anderson, R. C., Mansi, S. A., & Reeb, D. M. (2003). Founding family ownership and the agency cost of debt. *Journal of Financial Economics, 68*(2), 263–285.

Astrachan, J. C., & Jaskiewicz, P. (2008). Emotional returns and emotional costs in privately held family businesses: Advancing traditional business valuation. *Family Business Review, 21*, 139–149.

Astrachan, J. H., Klein, S. B., & Smyrnios, K. X. (2002). The F-PEC scale of family influence: A proposal for solving the family business definition problem. *Family Business Review, 15*(1), 45–58.

Bacci, S., Cirillo, A., Mussolino, D., & Terzani, S. (2017). The influence of family ownership dispersion on debt level in privately held firms. *Small Business Economics*, 1–20.

Barontini, R., & Caprio, L. (2006). The effect of family control on firm value and performance, evidence from continental Europe. *European Financial Management, 12*(5), 689–723.

Benavides-Velasco, C. A., Quintana-García, C., & Guzmán-Parra, V. F. (2013). Trends in family business research. *Small Business Economics, 40*(1), 41–57.

Bennedsen, M., & Nielsen, K. (2010). Incentive and entrenchment effects in European ownership. *Journal of Banking & Finance, 34*, 2212–2229.

Berrone, P., Cruz, C., Gómez-Mejía, L. R., & Larraza-Kintana, M. (2010). Socioemotional wealth and corporate responses to institutional pressures: Do family-controlled firms pollute less? *Administrative Science Quarterly, 55*(1), 82–113.

Berrone, P., Cruz, C., & Gómez-Mejía, L. R. (2012). Socioemotional wealth in family firms theoretical dimensions, assessment approaches, and agenda for future research. *Family Business Review, 25*, 258–279.

Boers, B., Ljungkvist, T., Brunninge, O., & Nordqvist, M. (2017). Going private: A socioemotional wealth perspective on why family controlled companies decide to leave the stock-exchange. *Journal of Family Business Strategy, 8*(2), 74–86.

Chirico, F., & Bau, M. (2014). Is the family an "asset" or "liability" for firm performance? The moderating role of environmental dynamism. *Journal of Small Business Management, 52*(2), 210–225.

Chrisman, J. J., Chua, J. H., & Litz, R. A. (2004). Comparing the agency costs of family and non–family firms: Conceptual issues and exploratory evidence. *Entrepreneurship Theory and Practice, 28*(4), 335–354.

Cohen, D. A., & Zarowin, P. (2010). Accrual-based and real earnings management activities around seasoned equity offerings. *Journal of Accounting and Economics, 50*(1), 2–19.

Colli, A., Pérez, P. F., & Rose, M. B. (2003). National determinants of family firm development? Family firms in Britain, Spain, and Italy in the 19th and 20th centuries. *Enterprise & Society, 4*(1), 28–64.

Cruz, C., Justo, R., & De Castro, J. O. (2012). Does family employment enhance MSEs performance?: Integrating socioemotional wealth and family embeddedness perspectives. *Journal of Business Venturing, 27*(1), 62–76.

European Commission. (2015). *Promoting entrepreneurship: Family business—Main challenges faced by family firms*. Retrieved from http://ec.europa.eu/growth/smes/promoting-entrepreneurship/we-work-for/family-business/index_en.htm

Fahlenbrach, R. (2009). Founder-CEOs, investment decisions, and stock market performance. *Journal of Financial and Quantitative Analysis, 44*(2), 439–466.

Fan, Q. (2007). Earnings management and ownership retention for initial public offering firms: Theory and evidence. *Accounting Review, 82*(1), 27–64.

Ferramosca, S., & Ghio, A. (2018). Earnings management in family firms. In *Accounting choices in family firms* (pp. 103–138). Cham: Springer.

Franks, J., Mayer, C., Volpin, P., & Wagner, H. F. (2011). The life cycle of family ownership: International evidence. *Review of Financial Studies, 25*(6), 1675–1712.

Gavana, G., Gottardo, P., & Moisello, A. M. (2017). Sustainability reporting in family firms: A panel data analysis. *Sustainability, 9*(1), 38.

Ghosh, A. A., & Moon, D. (2010). Corporate debt financing and earnings quality. *Journal of Business Finance & Accounting, 37*(5–6), 538–559.

Gomez-Mejia, L. R., Welbourne, T. M., & Wiseman, R. M. (2000). The role of risk sharing and risk taking under gainsharing. *Academy of Management Review, 25*(3), 492–507.

Gómez-Mejía, L. R., Haynes, K. T., Nunez-Nickel, M., Jacobson, K. J. L., & Moyano-Fuentes, J. (2007). Socioemotional wealth and business risks in family-controlled firms: Evidence from Spanish olive oil mills. *Administrative Science Quarterly, 52*, 106–137.

Gómez-Mejía, L. R., Makri, M., & Larraza-Kintana, M. (2010). Diversification decisions in family-controlled firms. *Journal of Management Studies, 47*, 223–252.

Gómez-Mejía, L. R., Cruz, C., Berrone, P., & De Castro, J. (2011). The bind that ties: Socioemotional wealth preservation in family firms. *Academy of Management Annals, 5*, 653–707.

Gómez-Mejía, L. R., Campbell, J. T., Martin, G., Hoskisson, R. E., Makri, M., & Sirmon, D. G. (2014a). Socioemotional wealth as a mixed gamble: Revisiting family firm R&D investments with the behavioral agency model. *Entrepreneurship Theory and Practice, 38*(6), 1351–1374.

Gómez-Mejía, L. R., Cruz, C., & Imperatore, C. (2014b). Financial reporting and the protection of socioemotional wealth in family-controlled firms. *European Accounting Review, 23*(3), 387–402.

Gómez-Mejía, L. R., Patel, P. C., & Zellweger, T. M. (2018). In the horns of the dilemma: Socioemotional wealth, financial wealth, and acquisitions in family firms. *Journal of Management, 44*(4), 1369–1397.

Gottardo, P., & Moisello, A. (2014). The capital structure choices of family firms: Evidence from Italian medium-large unlisted firms. *Managerial Finance, 40*(3), 254–275.

Handler, W. C. (1989). Methodological issues and considerations in studying family businesses. *Family Business Review, 2*(3), 257–276.

Huybrechts, J., Voordeckers, W., & Lybaert, N. (2013). Entrepreneurial risk taking of private family firms: The influence of a nonfamily CEO and the moderating effect of CEO tenure. *Family Business Review, 26*(2), 161–179.

Kotlar, J., Signori, A., De Massis, A., & Vismara, S. (2018). Financial wealth, socioemotional wealth, and IPO underpricing in family firms: A two-stage gamble model. *Academy of Management Journal, 61*(3), 1073–1099.

Leitterstorf, M. P., & Rau, S. B. (2014). Socioemotional wealth and IPO underpricing of family firms. *Strategic Management Journal, 35*(5), 751–760.

Liu, Y., Ning, Y., & Davidson III, W. N. (2010). Earnings management surrounding new debt issues. *Financial Review, 45*(3), 659–681.

Martin, G., Campbell, J. T., & Gómez-Mejía, L. R. (2016). Family control, socioemotional wealth and earnings management in publicly traded firms. *Journal of Business Ethics, 133*(3), 453–469.

McConaughy, D. L., Matthews, C. H., & Fialko, A. S. (2001). Founding family controlled firms: Performance, risk, and value. *Journal of Small Business Management, 39*(1), 31–49.

Migliori, S., Maturo, F., & Paolone, F. (2018). Capital structure determinants in family firms: An empirical analysis in context of crisis. *International Business Research, 11*(4), 65.

Miralles-Marcelo, J. L., del Mar Miralles-Quirós, M., & Lisboa, I. (2014). The impact of family control on firm performance: Evidence from Portugal and Spain. *Journal of Family Business Strategy, 5*(2), 156–168.

Morck, R., Shleifer, A., & Vishny, R. W. (1988). Management ownership and market valuation: An empirical analysis. *Journal of Financial Economics, 20*, 293–315.

Muñoz-Bullon, F., Sanchez-Bueno, M. J., & Suárez-González, I. (2017). Diversification decisions among family firms: The role of family involvement and generational stage. *BRQ Business Research Quarterly, 21*(1), 39–52.

Naldi, L., Chirico, F., Kellermanns, F. W., & Campopiano, G. (2015). All in the family? An exploratory study of family member advisors and firm performance. *Family Business Review, 28*(3), 227–242.

Pazzaglia, F., Mengoli, S., & Sapienza, E. (2013). Earnings quality in acquired and nonacquired family firms: A socioemotional wealth perspective. *Family Business Review, 26*(4), 374–386.

Prencipe, A., Markarian, G., & Pozza, L. (2008). Earnings management in family firms: Evidence from R&D cost capitalization in Italy. *Family Business Review, 21*(1), 71–88.

Rangan, S. (1998). Earnings management and the performance of seasoned equity offerings. *Journal of Financial Economics, 50*(1), 101–122.

Romano, C. A., Tanewsky, G. A., & Smyrnios, K. X. (2000). Capital structure decision making: A model for family business. *Journal of Business Venturing, 16*, 285–310.

Roosenboom, P., van der Goot, T., & Mertens, G. (2003). Earnings management and initial public offerings: Evidence from the Netherlands. *International Journal of Accounting, 38*(3), 243–266.

Sciascia, S., Mazzola, P., & Kellermanns, F. W. (2014). Family management and profitability in private family-owned firms: Introducing generational stage and the socioemotional wealth perspective. *Journal of Family Business Strategy, 5*(2), 131–137.

Shanker, M. C., & Astrachan, J. H. (1996). Myths and realities: Family businesses' contribution to the US economy–A framework for assessing family business statistics. *Family Business Review, 9*(2), 107–123.

Shivakumar, L. (2000). Do firms mislead investors by overstating earnings before seasoned equity offerings? *Journal of Accounting and Economics, 29*(3), 339–371.

Stockmans, A., Lybaert, N., & Voordeckers, W. (2010). Socioemotional wealth and earnings management in private family firms. *Family Business Review, 23*(3), 280–294.

Teoh, S. H., Welch, I., & Wong, T. J. (1998). Earnings management and the underperformance of seasoned equity offerings. *Journal of Financial Economics, 50*(1), 63–99.

Vandekerkhof, P., Steijvers, T., Hendriks, W., & Voordeckers, W. (2015). The effect of organizational characteristics on the appointment of nonfamily managers in private family firms: The moderating role of socioemotional wealth. *Family Business Review, 28*(2), 104–122.

Vieira, E. F. S. (2014). The effect on the performance of listed family and non-family firms. *Managerial Finance, 40*(3), 234–253.

Villalonga, B., & Amit, R. (2006). How do family ownership, control and management affect firm value? *Journal of Financial Economics, 80*, 385–417.

Voordeckers, W., Le Breton-Miller, I., & Miller, D. (2014). In search of the best of both worlds: Crafting a finance paper for the family business review. *Family Business Review, 27*(4), 281–286.

Wiseman, R. M., & Gomez-Mejia, L. R. (1998). A behavioral agency model of managerial risk taking. *Academy of Management Review, 23*(1), 133–153.

Zellweger, T. M., Kellermanns, F. W., Chrisman, J. J., & Chua, J. H. (2011). Family control and family firm valuation by family CEOs: The importance for intentions for transgenerational control. *Organization Science, 23*, 851–868.

Chapter 2
Family Control and Capital Structure Choices

Abstract This empirical study analyses the effect of family governance on family firms financing behavior. It combines elements of the capital structure theories with the socioemotional wealth approach (SEW), linking the emotional endowment of firm governance and the financing behavior. Using a dataset of 2986 private and listed Italian medium-large firms over the period 2001–2010, we show that family control and influence, as key dimension of the SEW, shapes a firm's capital structure choices. Multiple family members on the board and in executive positions, generational stage and ownership dispersion explain the results. A multiple presence of family members on the board and in executive positions has a signaling value for creditors. Moreover, we find that family businesses leverage is significantly affected by tangibility, legal structure, firm's market share and the sensibility to credit restrictions.

Keywords Family control · Family influence · Leverage · Capital structure choice · Ownership dispersion

2.1 Introduction

Family business studies have been growing during the last decades (Chrisman et al. 2008), and their financial choices are a quite unexplored area (Chen et al. 2014) which is arousing great interest among scholars (Michiels and Molly 2017). Many theories of capital structure have been offered to investigate the peculiarities of family business choices with Pecking order theory (POT) (Myers and Majluf 1984) and Trade-off theory (TOT) (DeAngelo and Masulis 1980; Titman 1984) the most widely accepted. TOT bases on costs related to information asymmetries between shareholders and lenders as well as debt related financial benefits. In doing so it takes into account, on the one hand, potential bankruptcy costs, on the other hand, benefits resulting from interests' deductibility. So, TOT assumes that financing decisions

P. Gottardo, A. M. Moisello, *Capital Structure, Earnings Management, and Risk of Financial Distress*, SpringerBriefs in Business,
https://doi.org/10.1007/978-3-030-00344-9_2

pursue an optimal capital structure that maximizes the value of a firm. POT bases on the information asymmetries between shareholders and different types of capital providers and it claims that firms follow a hierarchy of retained earnings, borrowing and equity issues. Family businesses are characterized by the overlap and interaction between the emotion-oriented family system and the financial result-oriented business system (Distelberg and Sorenson 2009). Koropp et al. (2014) point out that extant research on family firms financing choices has relied on a merely descriptive approach or on normative capital structure theories, focusing mostly on business factors and failing to account for family firms' preferences. Literature highlights the need of adjustments to standard finance models for a family effect (McConaughy 1999), suggesting that family firms' payout, growth and debt choices are led by strategic as well as emotional components, and family firm owners can accept lower financial returns in order to get non-monetary returns (Zellweger 2007). Families are more concerned by the risk of losing emotional and social benefits related to the business than with performance hazard (Gómez-Mejía et al. 2007). Empirical studies have found evidence of POT and shown different financing behavior between family and non-family businesses (Coleman and Carsky 1999; Mahérault 2000; Anderson et al. 2003; Lopez-Gracia and Sanchez-Andujar 2007; King and Santor 2008; Setia-Atmaja et al. 2009; Ellul 2010; Croci et al. 2011). Anderson and Reeb (2003a) analyzed the link between the level of debt and the risk aversion of family businesses. Research has found evidence of the effect on leverage of management ownership dispersion (Morck et al. 1988; Schulze et al. 2003), a firm's generational stages (Blanco-Mazagatos et al. 2007) and succession (Molly et al. 2010).

Family firms' financing decisions originate from both economic and non-economic motivations (Chrisman et al. 2004) therefore POT and TOT fails to explain the differences in leverage between family and non-family firms and among family businesses. Scholars call for studies to highlight and explain the heterogeneity of family businesses, moving beyond the emphasis on family firms as a unitary entity (Gómez-Mejía et al. 2011). Therefore, it is of interest to analyze how different forms of family influence on the business affect a firm's financing decisions.

The main objective of this chapter is to explain leverage levels of family firms. It argues that differences in financial structure between family and non-family firms, and among family firms, are affected by family owners' non-financial utilities and by the moderating effect that some characteristics of the firm have on these, i.e. listing, family involvement in management and on the board, ownership dispersion, and generational stage. We draw on the Socioemotional wealth framework, focalizing on the dimension related to family control and influence.

In order to do this, we analyze a dataset of 2986 private and listed medium-large Italian firms, over the period 2001–2010. Our findings are consistent with the POT theory, but the main implication of our results is that the family nature of businesses has a strong impact on a firm's attitude towards leverage. This is strengthened by family involvement in governance and by the first generational stage; it is weakened by ownership dispersion, regardless of listing.

The remainder of the chapter is structured as follows: the next section presents the literature review and the hypothesis development. The third section provides information on the data sample, the variables and the econometric methodologies applied. In the fourth section we present the empirical results and report the robustness checks. The section that follows discusses the results, highlights the limitations of this study, summarizes the contributions and implications for practice. Finally, in section six suggests some avenues for future research, we conclude.

2.2 Background and Hypothesis Development

Empirical studies suggest that family firms pursue conservative financial strategies (e.g. Caprio et al. 2011), that are affected by generational influences (Molly et al. 2012) and managerial succession (Amore et al. 2011). Family companies prefer internal financing (Romano et al. 2000), they merge personal and business resources in order to avoid external financing (Yilmazer and Schrank 2006), and, often, renounce to grow if this involves issuing equity capital (Mahérault 2004). Lopez-Gracia and Sanchez-Andujar (2007) tested POT versus static TOT in Spanish family and non-family small businesses and found results consistent with POT, coherent with previous studies such as Coleman and Carsky (1999) and Mahérault (2000). Blanco-Mazagatos et al. (2007) analyze agency costs against generation and desire to keep family control for a sample of Spanish firms; their results are coherent with POT predictions, and show that in second and subsequent generations family firms rely more on debt.

Nevertheless, the empirical literature on family firms financing behavior provides mixed results: some studies suggest that family firms use less debt (Margaritis and Psillaki 2010; Ampenberger et al. 2012, 2013; Schmid 2013) or use similar levels of debt as non-family firms (Anderson and Reeb 2003a), while the results of more numerous studies (e.g. Anderson et al. 2003; King and Santor 2008; Setia-Atmaja et al. 2009; Ellul 2010; Croci et al. 2011; Gottardo and Moisello 2014; Ramalho et al. 2018) indicate that family firms are more levered than non-family companies. These contrasting results may be affected by the different definition of family firms used (Westhead and Cowling 1998). This is related to the heterogeneity among the family firms, which are characterized by different degrees of family involvement in governance and management and value emotional and social benefits differently. Moreover, these mixed results may be due to the impact of the institutional context and of cultural differences on firms' financing behavior, resulting in a different propensity to open up the company to external equity capital depending on the country (Franks et al. 2011). In the case of family businesses, the propensity to open up the capital to outsiders cannot be explained only by financial reasons. Family firms are motivated by non-financial goals and the literature has pointed out the effect of the emotional connections family owners feel for their business on the psychological, behavioral, social and cognitive aspects of running the business (Sharma, 2004; Björnberg and Nicholson 2007; Astrachan and Jaskiewicz 2008; Chirico and Salvato 2008), the importance of family values as pillars of the family firm's culture (Aronoff 2004), the conservation of the family's social capital (Arrègle et al. 2007) and the altruistic behavior displayed by family owners oriented towards the family welfare.

According to the SEW perspective, family firms' behavior is aimed at increasing or preserving the stock of affect-related value invested in the business (Gómez-Mejía et al. 2007). SEW is a broad construct gathering different non-financial aspects of the business that meet the family's emotional needs (Gómez-Mejía et al. 2010). The utility the family derives from non-financial aspects of the business includes desire for family control and influence, identification of family members with the firm, preserving binding social ties between family members, emotional attachment of family members, and dynastic succession (Berrone et al. 2012; Gómez-Mejía et al. 2011).

Decision makers at family firms address risk in order to avoid losses of the accumulated endowment (Chrisman and Patel 2012). They are willing to make choices that jeopardize the financial performance, but on the other hand when performance is below target they avoid high variance investment which might bring performance closer to target (Gómez-Mejía et al. 2007) as the bankruptcy of the firm would result in the loss of the family wealth, both economic and non-economic. Gómez-Mejía et al. (2007, p. 108) propose that preserving the family firm's SEW "represents a key goal in and of itself. In turn, achieving this goal requires continued family control of the firm", so family firms exhibit a greater preference for control than non-family firms.

Family members are strongly linked to the firm, so family influence and control over the business is a key source of emotional satisfaction. Therefore, the importance of the family pursuit of socioemotional wealth and the power and sense of legitimacy by which the family implements decisions to increase this endowment, depends on the extent of family control through ownership (Zellweger et al. 2011).

The family feels a sense of identity and strong emotional ties with the firm, which is seen by internal and external stakeholders as an extension of the family itself (Berrone et al. 2012). Family firms not only try to avoid financing decisions that may dilute their control stakes but avoid opening up the capital to outside investors (Romano et al. 2000) as maintaining ownership strictly in the hands of the family keeps strangers out of the business and protects the sense of identity.

Ownership control is the means to defend and improve the family status, reputation, visibility and reciprocal bonds with a wide set of constituencies, such as employees, suppliers and lenders, as well as enhancing social relations with the community (Berrone et al. 2012; Gómez-Mejía et al. 2011). These links, that form a firm's social capital (Arrègle et al. 2007), meet family members' affective needs for belonging and develop the family's sense of legacy so that family owners perceive the loss of the company as a strong emotional experience (Sharma and Manikuti, 2005).

Families protect their ownership stakes as they view the firm as a long-term investment; a social capital to preserve (Colli 2012), an asset to be passed to future generations (Chami 2001) so as to renew the family ties to the firm through dynastic succession (Berrone et al. 2010, 2012). They avoid venturing risk, they do not pursue high growth risky investments (Gómez-Mejía et al. 2007) and are less likely to increase asset substitution or overinvestment (Hillier et al. 2018). There is also evidence that family firms are less prone to engage in earnings management (Martin et al. 2016) because of their reputational concerns (Gavana et al. 2017; Cennamo et al. 2012). For these reasons, family firms are considered better borrowers, they rely on an easier access to long term debt (Croci et al. 2011) as shown by their longer debt maturity structure (Díaz-Díaz et al. 2016). There is also evidence that debt contract strictness is less severe for family firms (Hillier et al. 2018), contracts are more favorable in terms of loans spread (Yen et al. 2015), the cost of debt is lower (Anderson et al. 2003; Ma et al. 2017), therefore family control enhances the speed of adjustment toward target leverage (Pindado et al. 2015).

On the one hand, family firms in their capital structure decisions may rely on better debt financing conditions; on the other hand, the future benefits of control are considered as part of the current emotional wealth and the intention for transgenerational control influences family owners' perception of the value of the firm's equity (Zellweger et al. 2011). In presence of socioemotional wealth utility, the value perceptions of family owners differ from market valuation as determined only by financial information (Zellweger and Astrachan 2008), and it suggests that their evaluation of optimal leverage takes into account these non-economic aspects which affect their perception of leverage risk.

Family control and influence is a source of emotional wealth itself and is the means that families have to preserve the stock of affective endowments in the firm in terms of influence, sense of identity, social ties, and link with future generations. Consequently, family firms should be more prone to use debt financing than non-family firms and pursue more strictly the POT hierarchy. The relevance of the "family control and influence" dimension depends on the percentage of shares hold by a family and we expect that the degree of family ownership is positively related to leverage, and it reinforces POT hierarchy.

H1 Family ownership stake is positively related to leverage ratio

The direct involvement of the family in the business in terms of the presence of a family CEO and/or of multiple family members on the board enhances the sense of identification between the family and the firm. A family CEO is more likely to avoid strategic decisions that could jeopardize the socioemotional wealth as he/she shares a common sense of identity with the family and is inclined to meet its desires and needs (Berrone et al. 2010; Gómez-Mejía et al. 2011). He/she may strengthen family's social ties using boards appointments (Bettinelli 2011) as non-family members are generally chosen based on trust relationship (Calabrò and Mussolino 2013). The CEO is rewarded with a relatively assured job, with the protection of the family from the risks related to the pursuit of goals other than profit maximization and reduced compensation risk (Gómez-Mejía et al. 2003). When a firm is led by a family CEO the image of the family and the company are more strictly related, and the reputational concern is more salient (Zellweger et al. 2013). Therefore, the motivation for complying with debt commitments should be stronger and it should improve the relations with lenders. Consistently Lardon et al. (2017), analyzing a sample of Belgian privately held family firms, found that non-family CEOs are more prone to take entrepreneurial risk but the companies they manage present a lower leverage than those led by a family CEO.

The link between the business and the family depends on different governance conditions, among which the number of family members on the board. The board is seen by the controlling family as a tool to strengthen its influence and control, legitimize the appointment and retention of senior executives and induce top executives to pursue the family's endowment preservation (Gómez-Mejía et al. 2011). The 'embeddedness' of the business within a family is characterized by the presence of family members, their power, and by their incentive for interaction, chief among them being the number of family members working there (Le Breton-Miller et al. 2011, p. 707). The presence of numerous family members on the board results in a more participative decision process (De Massis et al. 2014), enhances family identification, influence and personal investment in the business, increasing their endowment in the firm and the need to protect it; thereby retaining control.

Moreover, Arrègle et al. (2007) suggest that family involvement helps the family firm to obtain external financing by exploiting the social ties between family members and lenders. A multiple presence of the family on the board, and a family CEO, shows the presence of family members willing to keep control and the intention for transgenerational control impacting on the Socioemotional value (Zellweger et al. 2011). The sense of continuity with future generations, and long-term orientation, produces connections, binding social ties due to the existence of strong relationships with external stakeholders, among them external financiers (Haynes et al. 1999). Chua et al. (2011), studying new ventures capability of raising debt capital, found that family involvement enhances a new firm's ability to borrow family social capital to improve the relationship with lenders and enhance the likelihood of getting a third party's guarantee. This suggest that family involvement acts as a proxy for social capital (Hillier et al. 2018). There is evidence that during the crisis credit contracted less severely for family than non-family companies (Crespí and Martín-Oliver 2015), because of the additional soft information loan officers gathered through personal interactions with family firms managers (D'Aurizio et al. 2015).

In sum, family influence on management, in terms of a family CEO and the presence of multiple family members on the board, on the one hand facilitate the relations with lenders, and by its means debt raising, on the other hand it increases the endowment, the power and legitimacy by which the family pursues emotional and social benefits. So, it should increase the control motivation and, consequently, strengthen the hierarchy between debt and equity financing for family businesses.

H2 Family involvement in the business is positively related to leverage ratio

The family effect on leverage may differ according to a firm's generational stage as this affects the relevance of the SEW (Gómez-Mejía et al. 2011). SEW salience is highest in the earlier generational stages and, accordingly, the willingness to retain family control is strongest (Gómez-Mejía et al. 2007). In the first generation, companies are more likely to prioritize family's objectives over business goals (Westhead 2003). During this generational stage a firm is generally owned by the founding family and led by the founder, who has a strong motivation to preserve family control and to ensure the durability of the firm for the next generation and renew the family link to the business through succession (Berrone et al. 2012). The firm is "as an extension of themselves-their identity, or self-view" for founder-CEOs (Dyer and Whetten 2006) and they are less likely to open capital to non-family shareholders.

In the first generational stage strong emotional ties characterize the relation between the CEO and the other family members, so family's conflicts and pressures, that can modify a firm's preference between non-financial and financial goals, as well as harm a company's repayment capacity, are less likely to occur (Le Breton-Miller and Miller 2013). In later generational stages different family branches emerge, they may be conflicting and external directors, more financial goals oriented, might be appointed in order to moderate conflicts (Voordeckers et al. 2007).

Given the strong control motivation perceived by the founder we expect a higher preference for leverage during the first generational stage.

H3 Generational stage affects family firms' leverage ratio

Listing decision is a "mixed gamble" for family firms as they have to assess contrasting financial and socioemotional wealth factors (Gomez-Mejia et al. 2014). On the one hand, when a firm goes public, the owning family may rely on an increased personal financial liquidity, on financial incentives for managers, on a higher visibility as well as facilitation in succession (Boers et al. 2017). On the other hand, family owners have an accumulated endowment in the firm and they act in order to preserve it but "publicly listed companies are subject to scrutiny that limits how much family owners can pursue SEW objectives at the expense of public shareholders" (Le Breton-Miller and Miller 2013, p. 1396). Listing implies a series of formal constraints and requirements that affect firm's governance and management and influences family attitude in preserving the Socioemotional wealth (Naldi et al. 2013). Listed companies face a greater demand for disclosure, also related to strategic decisions (Anderson and Reeb 2003b). Miller et al. (2013) suggest that listed family businesses are more subject to institutional pressure as family visibility is especially prominent in large public firms and involvement in ownership and management is viewed with suspicion by outside stakeholders because they expect the family to pursue SEW. So, families need greater legitimacy to provide emotional and social benefits and they would include non-family members on the board and pursue conformity in the firm's strategic behavior in order to compensate governance peculiarities and garner legitimacy and status among outside stakeholders and the business community (Miller et al. 2013).

Listing implies a qualified presence of non-family shareholders and the owning family cannot influence their selection (Ravasi and Marchisio 2003). The presence of non-family shareholders has a moderating effect on SEW because the family must limit the propensity to pursue non-financial aspects of the business in order to meet other investors' expectations (Gómez-Mejía et al. 2011). Family owners perceive conflict with non-family stakeholders as detrimental to image and reputation (Berrone et al. 2010). Therefore, they must accept a compromise, i.e. limiting the pursuit of affective endowments to avoid bigger losses of SEW (Gomez-Mejia et al. 2014). Empirical literature shows that the ownership position of institutional investors influences family CEO compensation packages and discourages the awarding of firm stocks that would increase the power of the CEO to pursue the family agenda (Gómez-Mejía et al. 2003). Research shows that the effect of family control on a firm's investment decisions, such as R&D investments, is lower in the presence of institutional investors (Gomez-Mejia et al. 2014).

Moreover, listing modifies firms' financing possibilities and families' opportunities to maintain their endowment, enlarging the set of equity and debt-related instruments (Mahérault 2000; Amore et al. 2011). Shareholders of listed firms can increase the equity base, keeping control through rights issues, dual-class shares, preferred stocks, voting agreements and pyramidal control structures.

In short, listing should have a moderating effect on the pursuit of Socioemotional wealth and, of consequences, on the use of debt for control motivation, thus reducing the differences between listed family and non-family firms.

H4 Listing has a moderating effect on leverage of family firms

Prior empirical research (Agrawal and Nagarajan 1990; Friend and Lang 1988) shows that ownership dispersion has a positive effect on leverage. For family firms Schulze et al. (2003), find that ownership dispersion is positively related to debt, arguing that the board of firms in the cousin consortium stage tend to favor growth and, if they are unable to cut dividends or issue equity, are prone to use debt. When ownership is dispersed, shares are usually in the hands of the extended family members, most of them are not employed in the firm and have a passive attitude towards the business (Gersick 1997). Their approach is more comparable to those of institutional investors and non-family shareholders, they might be reluctant to wave their dividends to finance the business, risk taking behavior may change and show a preference for high growth risk investments that require financial resources, enhancing the use of debt (Schulze et al. 2003). Ownership dispersion among different family branches requires a more formal governance structure, in order to moderate conflicts, reducing the pursuit of non-financial goals and reducing the preference for family control and independence (Jaffe and Lane 2004). Family firms are most vulnerable to conflict and least willing to bear added risk, when ownership is splitted among family members (Schulze et al. 2003), suggesting that socioemotional wealth preservation, in terms of family harmony, should moderate the use of debt when this financing choice may exacerbate family conflicts (Gómez-Mejía et al. 2011).

Moreover, in case the dispersion of ownership across family owners with different roles, incentives and motivations has already brought conflicts, family members can't satisfy their needs for belonging, affect and intimacy within the firm. This reduces the noneconomic benefits that counterbalance the risk related to increased leverage. If conflicts related to different goals or to succession increase, the degree of family identification, influence and personal investment in the company changes (Gersick et al. 1997; Schulze et al. 2003; Gómez-Mejía et al. 2007; Le Breton-Miller and Miller 2013), lowering the control motivation in the use of debt financing.

Combining these arguments, we expect ownership dispersion to be positively related to debt but, given the moderating effect on Socioemotional wealth and, consequently, on the control motivation, we expect this effect to be lower for family firms.

H5 Ownership dispersion positively affect leverage ratio, but the effect is lower for family than for non-family firms

2.3 Research Methodology

2.3.1 Data

Our analysis is based on a dataset covering the period 2001–2010 extracted from AIDA (Italian Digital Database of Companies), the Italian provider of the Bureau van Dijk European Database. Our sample consists of non-financial firms that share the following characteristics: active in the year 2010 in the form of a limited company (S.r.l—Società a Responsabilità Limitata), or company limited by shares (S.p.a—Società per Azioni), and with revenues of over €70 million in at least 1 year.[1] The sample covers almost all medium-large private and listed Italian firms. We completed the database by entering the data on ownership and governance that is not in the AIDA database, using public filings from the Italian Chamber of Commerce Register.

The database contains 3086 private and listed firms; some of these have been deleted because the basic information necessary to construct some of the variables for the subsequent statistical analysis was missing. The usable sample includes financial information on 3009 firms but, through gathering the information on ownership and governance, we were able to classify as 'family' or 'non-family' firms only 2986 firms. Consequently, our final sample is made up of 1999 family firms and 987 non-family firms.

The classification of a firm as 'family' or 'non-family' is key. In studies based on questionnaires, the issue is often addressed by asking the respondents to classify their business by themselves, but respondents could have a different perception of what a family firm is. Solutions based on the presence of certain objective characteristics are therefore preferable. Briefly, the criteria could be based on ownership, management, the possibility to transfer the firm to the next generation, or some complex index of family influence (e.g., Westhead and Cowling 1998; McConaughy and Phillips 1999; Astrachan et al. 2002; Ampenberger et al. 2012). However, the variety of definitions is not restricted to private family firms as the same problem is also encountered in the listed firms literature (e.g., Anderson and Reeb 2003b; Villalonga and Amit 2010). Our primary discriminant between family and non-family firms is based on ownership. In the regression analysis, we control for the degree of family ownership, family involvement in the firm—measured in terms of active family management and presence of multiple family members on the board—and ownership dispersion. This approach allows us to verify if a closer degree of control and influence of the family has an impact on the leverage.

We define a listed family business as one where a family is the ultimate owner of the firm, assuming a minimum control threshold of 20%, while for a private family business we assume a minimum control threshold of 50%. This broad definition allows us to highlight the effect of different degrees of family involvement

[1]The threshold on revenues ensures the availability of the basic balance sheet items to carry out our analysis.

(ownership, board membership, management) on leverage. The threshold is consistent with those used in international studies of corporate ownership and facilitates the comparison of our results with those found previously. The threshold used in the literature in the case of listed firms ranges from 5% to 25% (Faccio and Lang 2002; Franks et al. 2011; Ellul 2010; Croci et al. 2011). In the case of private firms, a higher 50% cut-off is more usual (e.g. Lopez-Gracia and Sanchez-Andujar 2007; Amore et al. 2011) while for listed firms, with a dispersed ownership structure, a family, even with a limited stake of perhaps 20%, can exercise control on the firm. Nonetheless, our results are largely unaffected by the threshold choice: in fact, observing the data in Table 2.2, it is clearly evident that the ownership stake is very high in the family firms in our sample with a mean ownership of 93%.

Table 2.1 displays the profile of the firms in terms of size, age and industry. Family and non-family firms are well represented in all dimensional classes (assets in € millions) although family firms are relatively more numerous in the medium-low classes (under €90 million) while 55.1% of non-family firms belong to the larger

Table 2.1 Distribution of firms by size, age and industry

Panel A: total assets	All firms		Family		Non-family	
€ millions	Firms	%	Firms	%	Firms	%
< 10	57	1.9	46	2.3	11	1.1
10–50	888	29.7	660	33.3	228	23.1
50–90	758	25.4	554	27.7	204	20.7
> 90	1283	43.0	739	37.0	544	55.1
Panel B: age (years as of 2010)	All firms		Family		Non-family	
Years	Firms	%	Firms	%	Firms	%
< 10	512	17.1	287	14.3	225	22.8
10–20	622	20.8	344	17.2	278	28.2
20–30	695	23.3	503	25.2	192	19.4
30–40	578	19.4	479	24.0	99	10.0
> 40	579	19.4	386	19.3	193	19.6
Panel C: industry	All firms		Family		Non-family	
Sector	Firms	%	Firms	%	Firms	%
Apparel and textile	126	4.2	114	5.7	12	1.2
Wood and paper	72	2.4	56	2.8	16	1.6
Food and beverage	198	6.6	168	8.4	30	3.0
Heavy manufacturing	729	24.4	531	26.6	198	20.1
Chemicals, rubber and oil	349	11.7	203	10.2	146	14.8
Commerce	748	25.1	503	25.2	245	24.8
Construction	169	5.7	128	6.4	41	4.2
Communication	85	2.9	40	2.0	45	4.6
Electronic and electric equipment	148	5.0	74	3.7	74	7.5
Lodging, eating and amusement	64	2.1	38	1.9	26	2.6
Transportation	149	5.0	93	4.7	56	5.7
Utilities and business services	149	5.0	51	2.6	98	9.9

class. The firms are distributed fairly evenly across the different age classes. All industrial sectors are represented in the dataset though there are more heavy manufacturing and commerce companies, mirroring the structure of the Italian economy.

2.3.2 Variables

The dependent variable used in our descriptive statistics and regression models is Book Leverage, defined as the ratio of long-term and short-term financial debts to total assets (Rajan and Zingales 1995; Frank and Goyal 2009, Bennedsen and Nielsen 2010; Croci et al. 2011).

As for explanatory and control variables, we use Cash Flow, asset Tangibility, size, Liquidity: the literature indicates these factors in explaining capital structure choices (see Rajan and Zingales 1995; Lopez-Gracia and Sanchez-Andujar 2007; Frank and Goyal 2009; Ellul 2010; Michaelas et al. 1999; Schulze et al. 2003; Amore et al. 2011). We measure Cash Flow as the ratio of operational cash flow to total assets; Tangibility is the ratio of net property, plant and equipment to total assets. As a measure of size, we use the natural logarithm of sales—Ln(Sales). Liquidity is determined by the ratio of liquid assets to total assets; Family Ownership is the sum of the stakes owned by members of the family (Blanco-Mazagatos et al. 2007; Schulze et al. 2003; Bertrand et al. 2008; Romano et al. 2000).

To these variables, shown to be significant in previous research, we add: Firm's Market Share to control for firm"s market power (Gallo and Vilaseca 1996), Capital Turnover to control for the efficiency in the firm"s use of capital (Gallo et al. 2004), the Altman credit score to control for bankruptcy risk (Altman 1993) and, Banks Density as environmental variables (e.g. Becker et al. 2011). To measure a firm's market share, we match firms to industries requiring a non-missing ATECO code in the database and we determine market shares on firms' revenue basis. Capital turnover is the ratio of net sales to capital employed. The Altman Z' score is given by $Z' = 0{,}717X_1 + 0{,}847X_2 + 3{,}107X_3 + 0{,}420X_4 + 0{,}998X_5$ as in Altman et al. (2013), where the five ratios are respectively: net working capital, net income, operating income, equity, and sales all divided by total assets.

Banks Density is the number of banks branches per 100,000 people in the province where the business operates. Moreover, in the regression analysis we introduce several dummy variables: $D_{Foreign}$, which indicates whether the firm is controlled by a foreign firm, to control for the financing peculiarities of foreign affiliated firms (Desai et al. 2004); $D_{Legalstructure}$, to separate S.p.a from S.r.l companies to taking into account the legal structure impact; $D_{Industry}$ and D_{Year}, to control, respectively, the industry and year effects.

Families might use their control rights influencing the board through their voting rights, so family ownership (percentage of family held shares) is a measure of the indirect influence of the family on the business. Therefore, our main independent variable is Family Ownership, which is the sum of the percent stakes owned by members of the family in the firm. We use this variable as a measure of the "family influence and control" dimension of socioemotional wealth (Berrone et al. 2012).

According to our hypotheses we have four socioemotional wealth moderators: D_{Listed}, to distinguish listed and non-listed firms, $D_{Multi\text{-}ActiveFM}$, to distinguish the family firms with more than one family member on the board and at least one family member in an executive position; $D_{Dispersion}$, which indicates the firms in which none of the shareholders has an ownership stake of more than 50%, directly or indirectly; $D_{First\ Generational\ stage}$, which signals firms less than 25 years old. In line with Blanco-Mazagatos et al. (2007), we use this dummy variable to distinguish firms in the first generational stage because this cut off is around the time that second generation siblings enter the company (Xi et al. 2015).

2.3.3 Methods

We analyze the impact of family control on capital structure choices using several statistical approaches. We performed a preliminary correlation analysis to verify the absence of multicollinearity problems for our set of variables. Then we applied a cross-sectional analysis conducted by running distinct cross sections for each year of observation (from 2001 to 2010). However, cross-section methodology presents some limitations (Amore et al. 2011; Molly et al. 2010) that can be resolved using a panel data analysis. The panel data analysis uses efficiently cross and time-series data increasing the number of observations and the parameter"s reliability, reducing also the likelihood of multicollinearity problems. OLS standard errors are unbiased if the residuals are i.i.d. but, if the residuals are correlated across observations, OLS standard errors can be biased. To obtain more efficient estimates we perform a pooling analysis with standard errors adjusted for correlation within a cluster. In our methodology standard errors are clustered by firm. The resulting standard errors are unbiased and produce correct confidence intervals whether the firm effect is temporary or permanent (Petersen 2009). To control for time and industry fixed-effects we include dichotomous variables in the models. The correlations between the independent variables as well as the variance inflation factors are relatively small. We also analyzed the influence diagnostics to detect the presence of outliers. Three regression models are shown here: (1) control variables and the independent family ownership variable; (2) including the moderators; (3) adding the interaction variables. To verify the contribution of moderators and interaction variables we perform a hierarchical multiple regression analysis to test the R-squared improvement with respect to the base model (Aiken and West 1991).

2.4 Results and Robustness Checks

Table 2.2 presents descriptive statistics of the variables used in this study, distinguishing family and non-family firms.

Table 2.2 Descriptive statistics

		Family firms		Non-family firms		All firms	
		Mean	Stdev	Mean	Stdev	Mean	Stdev
1	Book leverage	25.81	17.73	18.76	18.06	23.45	18.13
2	Ln(Sales)	11.45	0.81	11.85	1.07	11.58	0.90
3	Firm market share	1.62	1.96	1.86	2.09	1.70	2.01
4	Cash flow	5.75	5.02	5.04	6.23	5.52	5.43
5	Family ownership	93.48	14.20	–	–	63.63	45.16
6	Liquidity	5.33	6.61	5.03	6.91	5.23	6.71
7	$D_{Legal\ structure}$	0.80	0.41	0.71	0.47	0.77	0.43
8	$D_{Foreign}$	8.42	29.58	55.02	50.80	23.92	43.86
9	$D_{Dispersion}$	0.25	0.45	0.20	0.42	0.24	0.44
10	D_{Listed}	0.02	0.17	0.01	0.15	0.02	0.16
11	$D_{Multi\text{-}Active\ FM}$	0.53	0.51	–	–	0.37	0.49
12	Altman score	3.22	3.29	3.78	3.70	3.41	3.44
13	$D_{First\ Generational\ Stage}$	0.48	0.51	0.66	0.48	0.54	0.51
	Firms	1999		987		2986	

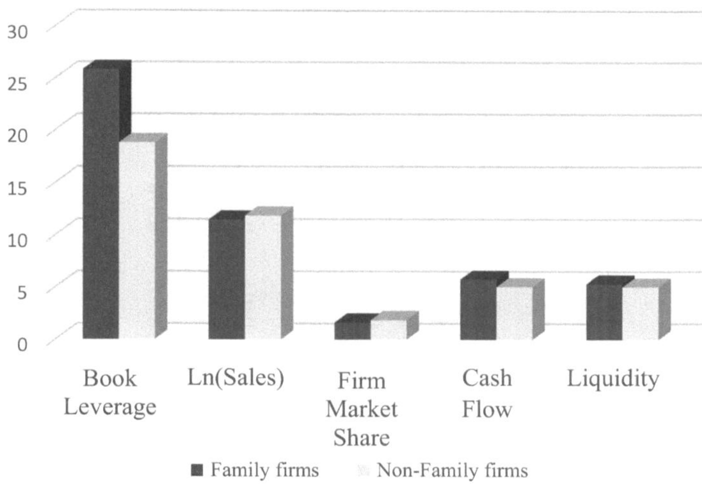

Fig. 2.1 Mean values: Family vs Non-Family firms

Family firms present higher leverage, liquidity and cash flow (Fig. 2.1). From the governance point of view, family firms show a very concentrated ownership. The family is well represented in active management; non-family firms are managed by professionals and a substantial part of them is held by a foreign entity not attributable to a family.

Table 2.3 presents the correlations analysis. Table 2.4 focuses on family firms and shows their characteristics in relation to the degree of family involvement, ranging

Table 2.3 Correlations

		1	2	3	4	5	6	7	8	9	10	11	12
1	Book leverage												
2	Ln(Sales)	**−0.078**											
3	Firm market share	**−0.126**	**0.078**										
4	Cash flow	**−0.180**	0.013	**0.074**									
5	Family ownership	**0.174**	**−0.227**	**−0.054**	**0.048**								
6	Liquidity	**−0.284**	**−0.097**	**0.046**	0.034	0.017							
7	$D_{Legal\ structure}$	**0.143**	**0.149**	**−0.054**	−0.003	**0.074**	**−0.061**						
8	$D_{Foreign}$	**−0.254**	**0.195**	**0.082**	−0.020	**−0.495**	**−0.042**	**−0.160**					
9	$D_{Dispersion}$	**0.163**	**−0.165**	−0.042	−0.001	**0.062**	0.020	**0.073**	**−0.277**				
10	D_{Listed}	−0.002	**0.128**	0.011	0.014	**−0.066**	0.009	**0.092**	**−0.080**	0.028			
11	$D_{Multi\text{-}Active\ FM}$	**0.229**	**−0.119**	**−0.086**	**0.047**	**0.480**	−0.034	**0.176**	**−0.415**	**0.220**	0.035		
12	Altman score	**−0.390**	**0.146**	0.018	**0.165**	**−0.091**	**0.231**	−0.030	**0.135**	**−0.066**	−0.034	**−0.057**	
13	$D_{First\ Generational\ Stage}$	−0.031	−0.009	0.007	**−0.070**	**−0.157**	**−0.065**	**−0.141**	**0.075**	**−0.062**	0.007	**−0.211**	−0.026

Bold indicates the correlation coefficients significant at the 5% level

Table 2.4 Involvement of family members in management and family firms characteristics. Mean values

	Zero FM in board	One FM No Exec	One FM Exec	More than one FM No Exec	One FM Exec and one or more FM No Exec
Book leverage	22.01	23.83	22.26	24.37	28.77
Ln(Sales)	11.63	11.66	11.22	11.65	11.43
Firm market share	1.77	2.00	1.82	1.72	1.46
Cash flow	4.72	6.33	5.91	6.14	5.84
Tangibility	14.91	16.92	16.38	14.48	17.91
Liquidity	4.87	3.83	6.59	6.20	5.05
Cost of debt	7.72	7.07	6.75	6.74	6.54
Family ownership	94.92	92.72	93.99	83.92	94.00
Firms foreign owned	41.37	13.54	2.03	3.81	0.93
Firm age	25	27	25	25	31
Executive board age	54	56	57	56	59
Firms	349	99	358	111	1082

from the class of firms where the family has no representation on the board to the class where the family has more members on the board and at least one executive.

The descriptive statistics suggest, in the case of family firms, consistently with Croci et al. (2011), a positive relationship between ownership involvement and leverage and, in line respectively with H2 and H3, this is particularly evident where a plurality of family members sits on the board and a firm is in the first generational stage, although the effect of the latter is not significantly different for family and non-family companies. We also notice that a consistent proportion of the firms with low family involvement have foreign ownership.

Capital structure choices are affected by management objectives: the distinctiveness of family firms is the family's desire to retain control while also avoid involving outside investors in the family business (Sirmon and Hitt 2003; Romano et al. 2000). These concerns could constrain growth (Coleman and Carsky 1999; Blanco-Mazagatos et al. 2007), in fact the family firms in our dataset are, on average, measured in total assets, less than a third the size of non-family businesses. Our sample firms are medium-large, therefore the families involved adopted financial policies which preserved control to ensure growth, by using debt (King and Santor 2008). Medium-large family firms generally show a higher leverage ratio which, however, does not reach pathological levels as these companies show, on average, a better capability to generate self-financing and liquidity.

To deal with the limitations of a cross-sectional analysis, we perform a panel-data analysis with standard error clustered at the firm level and we control for time and industry fixed-effect using dummy variables. Table 2.5 displays the results.

Consistent with Anderson et al. (2003), King and Santor (2008) and Setia-Atmaja et al. (2009), family ownership has a direct effect on leverage as shown by the significance of the Family Ownership coefficient in models 1 and 3. This result

Table 2.5 Pooling GLS regressions with clustered standard errors

Full sample, period 2001–2010	Model 1	Model 2	Model 3
Controls			
Intercept	0.17***	0.14***	0.13***
Ln(Sales)	0.00	0.00	0.00
Cash flow	−0.45***	−0.46***	−0.46***
Tangibility	0.09***	0.08***	0.08***
Firm market share	−0.79***	−0.66***	−0.66***
Liquidity	−0.48***	−0.46***	−0.46***
Capital turnover	−0.01**	−0.01***	−0.01***
Banks density	0.00***	0.00***	0.00***
$D_{Foreign}$	−0.09***	−0.06***	−0.06***
$D_{Legal\ structure}$	0.03***	0.02***	0.02***
Altman score	−0.01***	−0.01***	−0.01***
$D_{Industry}$	Yes	Yes	Yes
D_{Year}	Yes	Yes	Yes
Independent variable			
Family ownership	0.00***	0.00	0.00**
Moderators			
$D_{Dispersion}$		0.04***	0.06***
D_{Listed}		−0.03*	−0.03
$D_{Multi\text{-}Active\ FM}$		0.04***	0.04***
$D_{First\ Generational\ Stage}$		0.01*	0.02**
Family own x $D_{Dispersion}$			−0.00**
Family own x D_{Listed}			0.00
Family own x $D_{First\ Generational\ Stage}$			−0.00
Adjusted R^2	0.220	0.233	0.234
ΔR^2		0.013**	0.014**

***, **, * Indicate significance at the 1%, 5% and 10% level respectively

confirms the evidence of descriptive statistics, supports *H1* and is coherent with the findings of Ellul (2010) and Croci et al. (2011). Family firms are risk averse, as shown by their long term and low-risk investments (Naldi et al. 2007), and are characterized by long-term commitments so their higher leverage could be explained as a means of maintaining control. We find no evidence of a moderating effect of listing on leverage, the dummy D_{listed} and the interaction term coefficients are never significant and *H4* is not verified.

$D_{Multi\text{-}ActiveFM}$ is a complex indicator of the degree of family involvement. Within the firm, having multiple family members on the board and in executive positions increases the SEW and the embeddedness of the firm in the family increasing the use of debt. In addition, the personal relations of these members and the long tenure of a family CEO reinforce links with creditors. Regression results support *H2*, showing a positive and significant relationship between leverage ratio and the degree of family involvement. These findings are also consistent with the descriptive data in Table 2.4 which shows that firms with the highest family involvement present the highest leverage.

The panel data results show that higher ownership dispersion increases leverage for both family and non-family firms, but the effect is lower for family firms. This result supports *H5*. Consistent with Schulze et al. (2003) ownership dispersion has a positive effect on debt. In the case of family firms, this is both an indicator of ownership dispersion and dispersion among the family members, given the high level of family ownership, in our family subsample, as shown in Table 2.2.[2] The effect on leverage is weaker for family firms as shown by the negative coefficient of the interaction term and we interpret this as the result of the moderating role that family ownership dispersion has on SEW. These results extend those found by Morck et al. (1988) and Schulze et al. (2003) on the effect of managerial ownership dispersion.

Regarding the other control variables, the results obtained are consistent with those found in the capital structure literature. Cash Flow and Liquidity markedly affect leverage and the negative relationship, is consistent with POT predictions.[3] The evidence shows that Capital Turnover has a negative relation with leverage as a business with a higher turnover ratio requires fewer financial resources.

According with Nishihara and Shibata (2014) we find that a Firm's Market Share is always negatively related with leverage. In relation to the environmental variables, Banks Density is significant and positively related with leverage. Foreign ownership has a negative and significant effect on leverage. This result is peculiarly relevant in the case of family firms for two reasons: firstly, foreign ownership is related to international group membership and the financial policies of multinational firms have been shown to be different from those of domestic firms (Desai et al. 2004); secondly, foreign-owned family firms' governance is likely to be different to that of purely domestic family firms. This is particularly true when the firm is an affiliate of a multinational, as, in such cases, the management and governance styles approach those of non-family businesses.

As expected the Altman score is negatively related to leverage, the coefficient is always significant. Finally, the legal structure, i.e. the fact of being an S.p.a firm, has a positive and significant effect on leverage. S.p.a firms are subjected to a tighter set of regulations than S.r.ls and this legal structure is perceived by creditors as a tool that reduces the asymmetric information of family firms as well as agency costs.

---

[2]This is a very concise indicator of dispersion, so, in order to also take into account the number of owners, we modified the dummy variable assuming that it takes value 1 only once the data respects a joint condition: no shareholders hold more than 50% (direct or total) of the voting rights and the owners number is at least four. The (unreported) results with this different definition of the variable do not modify the effect and significance of ownership dispersion on leverage.

[3]The results in sub-sample analyses of family and non-family firms indicate that the effect is stronger for family than non-family firms.

Beyond those indicated in note (3), we perform three other sets of analysis to test the robustness of the empirical results found so far. A potential concern with the interpretation of our findings as a signal of causal relationship between leverage and the independent variables is that the regressions in Table 2.5 use contemporaneous observations. To deal with this concern we run the year-by-year cross sections and the pooling analyses using 1-year lagged family stakes and control variables: the above results still hold using 1-year lagged determinants and maintain their relevance both qualitatively and quantitatively. As a further check, we also run the pooling regression with clustered standard errors and the cross sections using 2-year lagged determinants obtaining similar results.

A second concern is the definition of family firm assumed, as different ownership thresholds could modify the results. We verified the robustness of our findings to the threshold using a common 20% threshold for both listed and private firms and a more conservative criterion with a common 50% threshold.

A third potential concern is related to the robustness of our findings to an alternative measure of leverage. So we repeated the regression analyses using another measure of leverage widely used in empirical literature (Lopez-Gracia and Sanchez-Andujar 2007; Molly et al. 2010; Amore et al. 2011) given by total debt over total assets. Overall the results show that if we modify the proxy for leverage we have limited effects on the estimated coefficients and significance.

A fourth potential concern with the results is the impact of omitted relevant factors, independent of the amount of exploratory data analysis we carried out. There is some other potentially relevant determinant that could impact our results and that should be taken into account. One possibility is to introduce an indicator of the demand and/or supply of credit. The global recession triggered by the 2007 financial crisis severely limited the possibility of firms to borrow from lenders and the resulting shrinkage of credit supply (credit crunch) could show up in our data and influence our findings. To verify if, and to what extent, the credit shortage in the last few years covered by our analyses drives the results, we modified the panel data models introducing as a control variable an indicator of credit supply restriction ($I_{CrOffer}$).[4] The panel results with standard errors clustered by firm are shown in Table 2.6. Credit supply restriction has a significant effect on firms, reducing leverage, but the introduction of this control variable does not modify in any significant way the effect and relevance of the other variables. We also performed a further check by substituting the credit supply indicator with the indicator of credit demand. It presented a positive relation with leverage and, as in the previous case, we do not find any significant change in the results for the other variables.

[4]To construct our yearly indicator we use the results of the quarterly Bank Landing Survey realized by the Bank of Italy and the other central banks in the Euro area. Unfortunately, the survey has existed since 2003, so, to carry out this analysis, we limit ourselves to the 2003–2010 period.

Table 2.6 Pooling GLS regressions with clustered standard errors

Leverage and credit supply. Full sample, period 2003–2010	Model 1	Model 2	Model 3
Controls			
Intercept	0.20***	0.16***	0.15***
Ln(Sales)	−0.00	0.00	0.00
Cash flow	−0.43***	−0.45***	−0.45***
Tangibility	0.08***	0.08***	0.08***
Firm market share	−0.87***	−0.75***	−0.76***
Liquidity	−0.46***	−0.45***	−0.45***
Capital turnover	−0.01**	−0.01***	−0.01***
Banks density	0.00***	0.00***	0.00***
$I_{CrOffer}$	−0.02***	−0.02***	−0.02***
$D_{Foreign}$	−0.09***	−0.07***	−0.06***
$D_{Legal\ structure}$	0.03***	0.03***	0.03***
Altman score	−0.01***	−0.01***	−0.01***
$D_{Industry}$	Yes	Yes	Yes
Independent variable			
Family ownership	0.00**	0.00	0.00**
Moderators			
$D_{Dispersion}$		0.04***	0.07***
D_{Listed}		−0.02	−0.03
$D_{Multi\text{-}Active\ FM}$		0.04***	0.04***
$D_{First\ Generational\ Stage}$		0.01**	0.02**
Family own x $D_{Dispersion}$			−0.00**
Family own x D_{Listed}			0.00
Family own x $D_{First\ Generational\ Stage}$			−0.00
Adjusted R^2	0.226	0.241	0.242
ΔR^2		0.015**	0.016**

***, ** Indicate significance at the 1% and 5% level respectively

2.5 Discussion

Consistently with prior research (Poutziouris 2001; Lopez-Gracia and Sanchez-Andujar 2007), our findings show that, overall, the leverage choices of medium-large Italian firms are consistent with POT predictions, but POT and TOT, taken separately, cannot explain the differences in capital structure between family and non-family firms and within family businesses. However, they have elements that, combined with the Socioemotional wealth approach, help explain many aspects of these firms' financing decisions. Firms' leverage shows a high sensitivity to variables related to self-financing capabilities such as cash flow and liquidity. Family firms present a higher self-financing capability and are more levered. Family firms high leverage is coherent with POT because after using self-financing they prefer to use debt in order to maintain control, as, according to Arrègle et al. (2007, p. 84), "family members are concerned about the firm because it is part of their collective patrimony and is often the main asset of the family".

Extant literature (McConaughy 1999; Adams et al. 2004; Zellweger 2007) argues that the relation between the family and the business has a lowering effect on a firm cost of capital affecting its investment and financing decisions; our study confirms a family effect on capital structure by the means of debt financing.

Family firms are not a unitary entity, our results show heterogeneous behaviors in financing decision. The identification of family businesses based on ownership allowed us to see how a different degree of control and influence of the family affects the preference for debt. Firms adhere more strictly to POT when the family influence, in term of family involvement in management, is higher and stronger socioemotional aspects impact on control motivations (Gómez-Mejía et al. 2007).

Our results show that family firms are prone to assume financial risk by increasing their leverage, as the assessment of risk takes into account also non-monetary benefits. This is consistent with the empirical findings of Gómez-Mejía et al. (2007) reporting that family owning olive oil mills prefer to be independent and not to join a cooperative giving up the related financial benefits and firm risk reduction. These results are also consistent with Zellweger (2007) that argues that family firms cost of capital is lower as their owners are free to substitute monetary with non-monetary returns, so family businesses prefer self-financing and then they prefer debt financing to equity. Family firms are risk adverse, but they may be also risk taking in order to preserve the owning family socioemotional wealth (Gómez-Mejía et al. 2007). Consistently, our findings indicate that family firms, during the first generational stage, when the socioemotional wealth is highest, present a higher leverage than during the subsequent stages.

The degree of family involvement in the business impacts on the stock of non-monetary benefits they count on and in so doing on their preference for debt. The degree of family control and influence also modifies the perception of risk and by its means leverage. Our findings suggest that the differences in leverage within family businesses, and between family and non-family firms, are related to the characteristics of family involvement in term of presence on the board and in executive positions and ownership dispersion. The presence of multiple family members on the board joint to at least a family member in executive position, on the one hand, raises family endowment and motivation to control. On the other hand social interactions between lenders and borrowers affect credit availability (Lehmann and Neuberger 2001; D'Aurizio et al. 2015), the presence of multiple family members on the board improves the opportunity to build more effective relationships with financial institutions due to the longer tenure of family CEO (Zellweger, 2007) and family network ties (Berrone et al. 2012; Arrègle et al. 2007; Sirmon and Hitt 2003). Our data also may suggest that the number of family members involved in the business also moderates the cost of debt. Our results confirm previous research (Schulze et al. 2003) as we find that ownership dispersion positively affects debt and they go beyond showing that the effect of the dispersion has a more moderate effect in the case of family businesses than for non-family firms. Moreover, our results suggest that listing doesn't affect significantly the leverage choices of Italian family firms and this is probably due to the families' viscosity in diluting control (Mengoli et al. 2009) and to the characteristics of the insider system in which they operate.

Our study shows that family firms' debt financing choices are complex and that the integration of capital structure and the SEW approach is crucial in understanding their behavior. Empirical evidence indicates that the financing behavior of medium and large family and non-family business is significantly different. We show that what is really important is not listing but the family nature of the business, its heterogeneity in terms of board characteristics and generational stage. These findings also confirm the relevance of other company characteristics, such as cash flow and investment structure. Firms' peculiarity in financing decisions is highlighted by the significance of their propensity to invest in physical assets, the legal structure and their sensitivity to credit supply restrictions. The firms positioning in their product market, and the competitive conditions of their industry, affects leverage showing that firms in stronger positions have less need to resort to debt.

2.6 Contributions and Implications

Our study contributes to the literature in several ways. We add to the family firm behavior literature by combining elements of the capital structure theories with the Socioemotional wealth approach and point out how these elements are intermingled and shape the financial decisions of Italian family firms, explaining the differences compared to non-family firms and between family businesses. We address calls to pay greater attention to the heterogeneity of family firms (Salvato and Moores 2010; Uhlaner et al. 2012), and to Gómez-Mejía et al. (2011) call to explore the family firms' decisions depending on their degree of SEW.

Our results have some implications for theory and practice. We contribute to theory suggesting that capital structure theories should be adapted for family firms taking into account the noneconomic aspects that lead their decisions. Standalone theories fail to fully interpret family businesses financial behavior. POT hierarchy fits to family firms but the preference for debt financing is graduated by noneconomic objectives which depend on the involvement of the family in terms of ownership and management. TOT assumes that firms pursue a target leverage ratio but in the case of family firms the non-financial utilities which family owners derives from the business modifies their risk perception and the use of debt financing.

Our results have some implications for regulators and family firms' stakeholders. The low liquidity of the Italian equity market, in terms of number of listed firms and capitalization, is noteworthy even with respect to other insider systems such as France and Germany; our results may help shed light on the causes of this phenomenon that is probably linked to Italian families' aversion to open up capital and share their endowment with outsiders. This could suggest the regulatory bodies to adopt measures that allow listed and private firms to issue shares with multiple voting rights, in order to reduce concerns about outsiders and stimulate the development of the equity market. Clearly, these measures must be accompanied by stronger investor protection and appropriate actions on the regulatory framework.

Another implication is the need for family firms' stakeholders and decision makers to be aware that in presence of emotional and social benefits families might have a biased perception of risk underestimating the financial hazard. They also need to be mindful that this attitude might be increased by the presence of a family CEO and multiple family members on the board. Moreover, our results may increase family awareness of the possible consequences of investments and legal structure decisions on their capability to raise debt capital.

2.6.1 *Limitations and Future Research*

This study presents some limitations. The first limitation is that we focus on debt financing and further research would extend the analysis to self-financing and equity.

The second limitation concerns the measurement of socioemotional wealth. As a proxy of its value we use the percentage of shares owned by a family because it is the only available alternative for studies based on large archival databases (Berrone et al. 2012). This variable catches the "family control and influence" dimension but is not able to capture other aspects such as sense of identity, intention of renewal family bonds to the firm through dynastic succession, relations within the owning family and between the family and other stakeholders. Hauck et al. (2016) have quite recently pointed out as a limit of extant literature that SEW dimensions are often measured indirectly through proxies such as family ownership and involvement. Further research could address this gap using different approaches such as surveys, content analysis and case studies in order to evaluate the impact of these other dimensions on financing choices. A multi-dimensional measurement of non-economic factors is required and the development, testing and validation of the SEW measurement and his impact on family firm decisions are important future research avenues (Miller and Le Breton-Miller 2014; Gómez-Mejía et al. 2011).

Another limit of this study is that it takes into account only four moderators of a family endowment, but we are well aware that other factors may have an effect on it modifying the control motivation and the inter-temporal preference of debt versus equity in family firms, such as firm hazard, qualified presence of non-family shareholders, family conflicts, CEOs' tenure, the intergenerational transfer of the business or the substitution of family with professional managers.

We show that product market characteristics and competitive conditions within an industry are an important determinant of the capital structure decisions and they need to be further investigated for family firms.

A further limitation of this study is that it focuses on a single country and it could be of interest to verify our results in an international setting.

References

Adams, A. F., Manners, G. E., Astrachan, J. H., & Mazzola, P. (2004). The importance of integrated goal setting: The application of cost of capital concepts to private firms. *Family Business Review, 17*, 287–302.

Agrawal, A., & Nagarajan, N. J. (1990). Corporate capital structure, agency costs and ownership control: The case of all-equity firms. *Journal of Finance, 45*, 1325–1331.

Aiken, L. S., & West, S. G. (1991). *Multiple regression: Testing and interpreting interactions*. Newbury Park, CA: Sage.

Altman, E. I. (1993). *Corporate financial distress*. New York: Wiley Interscience.

Altman, E. I., Danovi, A., & Falini, A. (2013). Z-score models' application to Italian companies subject to extraordinary administration. *Journal of Applied Finance, 23*, 114–128.

Amore, M. D., Minichilli, A., & Corbetta, G. (2011). How do managerial successions shape corporate financial policies in family firms? *Journal of Corporate Finance, 17*, 1016–1027.

Ampenberger, M., Bennedsen, M., & Zhu, H. (2012). The capital structure of family firms. In D. Cumming (Ed.), *Oxford handbook of entrepreneurial finance* (pp. 167–191). Oxford: Oxford University Press.

Ampenberger, M., Schmid, T., Achleitner, A. K., & Kaserer, C. (2013). Capital structure decisions in family firms: Empirical evidence from a bank-based economy. *Review of Managerial Sciences, 7*, 247–275.

Anderson, R. C., & Reeb, D. M. (2003a). Founding-family ownership, corporate diversification and firm leverage. *Journal of Law and Economics, 46*, 653–680.

Anderson, R. C., & Reeb, D. M. (2003b). Founding-family ownership and firm performance: Evidence from the S&P 500. *Journal of Finance, 58*, 1301–1328.

Anderson, R. C., Mansi, A. M., & Reeb, D. M. (2003). Founding family ownership and the agency cost of debt. *Journal of Financial Economics, 68*, 263–285.

Aronoff, C. (2004). Self-perpetuation family organizations built on values: Necessary conditions for long-term family business survival. *Family Business Review, 17*, 55–59.

Arrègle, J. L., Hitt, M., Sirmon, D., & Véry, P. (2007). The development of organizational social capital: Attributes of family firms. *Journal of Management Studies, 44*, 73–95.

Astrachan, J. C., & Jaskiewicz, P. (2008). Emotional returns and emotional costs in privately held family businesses: Advancing traditional business valuation. *Family Business Review, 21*, 139–149.

Astrachan, J. H., Klein, S. B., & Smyrnion, K. X. (2002). The F-PEC scale of family influence: A proposal for solving the family business definition problem. *Family Business Review, 15*, 45–58.

Becker, B., Cronqvist, H., & Fahlenbrach, R. (2011). Estimating the effects of large shareholders using a geographic instrument. *Journal of Financial and Quantitative Analysis, 46*, 907–942.

Bennedsen, M., & Nielsen, K. M. (2010). Incentive and entrenchment effects in European ownership. *Journal of Banking & Finance, 34*, 2212–2229.

Berrone, P., Cruz, C., Gómez-Mejía, L. R., & Larraza-Kintana, M. (2010). Socioemotional wealth and organizational response to institutional pressures: Do family controller firms pollute less? *Administrative Science Quarterly, 55*, 82–113.

Berrone, P., Cruz, C., & Gómez-Mejía, L. R. (2012). Socioemotional wealth in family firms theoretical dimensions, assessment approaches, and agenda for future research. *Family Business Review, 25*, 258–279.

Bertrand, M., Johnson, S., Samphantharak, K., & Schoar, A. (2008). Mixing family with business: A study of Thai business groups and the families behind them. *Journal of Financial Economics, 88*, 466–498.

Bettinelli, C. (2011). Boards of directors in family firms: An exploratory study of structure and group process. *Family Business Review, 24*, 151–169.

Björnberg, Å., & Nicholson, N. (2007). The family climate scales—Development of a new measure for use in family business research. *Family Business Review, 20*(3), 229–246.

Blanco-Mazagatos, F., de Quevedo-Puente, E., & Castrillo, L. A. (2007). The trade-off between financial resources and agency costs in the family business: An exploratory study. *Family Business Review, 20*, 199–213.
Boers, B., Ljungkvist, T., Brunninge, O., & Nordqvist, M. (2017). Going private: A socioemotional wealth perspective on why family controlled companies decide to leave the stock-exchange. *Journal of Family Business Strategy, 8*(2), 74–86.
Calabrò, A., & Mussolino, D. (2013). How do boards of directors contribute to family SME export intensity? The role of formal and informal governance mechanisms. *Journal of Management & Governance, 17*, 363–403.
Caprio, L., Croci, E., & Del Giudice, A. (2011). Ownership structure, family control, and acquisition decisions. *Journal of Corporate Finance, 17*, 1636–1657.
Cennamo, C., Berrone, P., Cruz, C., & Gómez-Mejía, L. R. (2012). Socioemotional wealth and proactive stakeholder engagement: Why family controlled firms care more about their stakeholders. *Entrepreneurship Theory and Practice, 36*, 1153–1173.
Chami, M. R. (2001). *What is different about family businesses?* (No. 1–70). International Monetary Fund.
Chen, T. Y., Dasgupta, S., & Yu, Y. (2014). Transparency and financing choices of family firms. *Journal of Financial and Quantitative Analysis, 49*(2), 381–408.
Chirico, F., & Salvato, C. (2008). Knowledge integration and dynamic organizational adaptation in family firms. *Family Business Review, 21*, 169–181.
Chrisman, J. J., Chua, J. H., & Litz, R. A. (2004). Comparing the agency cost of family and non-family firms: Conceptual issues and exploratory evidence. *Entrepreneurship Theory and Practice, 28*, 335–354.
Chrisman, J. J., Chua, J. H., Kellermanns, F. W., Matherne III, C. F., & Debicki, B. J. (2008). Management journals as venues for publication of family business research. *Entrepreneurship Theory and Practice, 32*(5), 927–934.
Chrisman, J. J., & Patel, P. C. (2012). Variations in R&D investments of family and nonfamily firms: Behavioral agency and myopic loss aversion perspectives. *Academy of Management Journal, 55*(4), 976–997.
Chua, J. H., Chrisman, J. J., Kellermanns, F., & Wu, Z. (2011). Family involvement and new venture debt financing. *Journal of Business Venturing, 26*(4), 472–488.
Coleman, S., & Carsky, M. (1999). Sources of capital for small family owned businesses: Evidence from the national survey of small business finances. *Family Business Review, 12*, 73–86.
Colli, A. (2012). Contextualizing performances of family firms. The perspective of business history. *Family Business Review, 25*, 243–257.
Crespí, R., & Martín-Oliver, A. (2015). Do family firms have better access to external finance during crises? *Corporate Governance: An International Review, 23*(3), 249–265.
Croci, E., Doukas, J. A., & Gonec, H. (2011). Family control and financing decisions. *European Financial Management, 17*, 860–897.
D'Aurizio, L., Oliviero, T., & Romano, L. (2015). Family firms, soft information and bank lending in a financial crisis. *Journal of Corporate Finance, 33*, 279–292.
De Massis, A., Chirico, F., Kotlar, J., & Naldi, L. (2014). The temporal evolution of proactiveness in family firms: The horizontal S-curve hypothesis. *Family Business Review, 27*, 35–50.
Deangelo, H., & Masulis, R. W. (1980). Optimal capital structure under corporate and personal taxation. *Journal of Financial Economics, 8*(1), 3–29.
Desai, M. A., Foley, C. F., & Hines, J. R. (2004). A multinational perspective on capital structure choice and internal capital markets. *Journal of Finance, 59*, 2451–2487.
Díaz-Díaz, N. L., García-Teruel, P. J., & Martínez-Solano, P. (2016). Debt maturity structure in private firms: Does the family control matter? *Journal of Corporate Finance, 37*, 393–411.
Distelberg, B., & Sorenson, R. L. (2009). Updating systems concepts in family businesses: A focus on values, resource flows, and adaptability. *Family Business Review, 22*(1), 65–81.
Dyer, W. G., & Whetten, D. A. (2006). Family firms and social responsibility: Preliminary evidence from the S&P 500. *Entrepreneurship Theory and Practice, 30*(6), 785–802.

Ellul, A. (2010). *Control motivations and capital structure decision* (Working paper). Bloomington, IN: Indiana University, Kelley School of Business.

Faccio, M., & Lang, L. H. P. (2002). The ultimate ownership of Western Europe corporations. *Journal of Financial Economics, 65*, 365–395.

Frank, M. Z., & Goyal, V. K. (2009). Capital structure decisions: Which factors are reliably important? *Financial Management, 38*, 1–37.

Franks, J., Mayer, C., Volpin, P., & Wagner, H. F. (2011). The life cycle of family ownership: International evidence. *Review of Financial Studies, 25*(6), 1675–1712.

Friend, I., & Lang, L. H. P. (1988). An empirical test of the impact of managerial self-interest on corporate capital structure. *Journal of Finance, 43*(2), 271–281.

Gallo, M. A., & Vilaseca, A. (1996). Finance in family business. *Family Business Review, 9*, 387–402.

Gallo, M. A., Tapies, J., & Capuins, K. (2004). Comparison of family and non-family business: Financial logic and personal preferences. *Family Business Review, 17*, 303–318.

Gavana, G., Gottardo, P., & Moisello, A. M. (2017). Earnings management and CSR disclosure. Family vs. non-family firms. *Sustainability, 9*(12), 2327.

Gersick, K. E. (Ed.). (1997). *Generation to generation: Life cycles of the family business*. Brighton, MA: Harvard Business Press.

Gómez-Mejía, L. R., Larraza-Kintana, M., & Makri, M. (2003). The determinants of executive compensation in family-controlled public corporations. *Academy of Management Journal, 46*, 226–237.

Gómez-Mejía, L. R., Haynes, K. T., Nunez-Nickel, M., Jacobson, K. J. L., & Moyano-Fuentes, J. (2007). Socioemotional wealth and business risks in family-controlled firms: Evidence from Spanish olive oil mills. *Administrative Science Quarterly, 52*, 106–137.

Gómez-Mejía, L. R., Makri, M., & Larraza-Kintana, M. (2010). Diversification decisions in family-controlled firms. *Journal of Management Studies, 47*, 223–252.

Gómez-Mejía, L. R., Cruz, C., Berrone, P., & De Castro, J. (2011). The bind that ties: Socioemotional wealth preservation in family firms. *Academy of Management Annals, 5*, 653–707.

Gomez-Mejia, L. R., Campbell, J. T., Martin, G., Hoskisson, R. E., Makri, M., & Sirmon, D. G. (2014). Socioemotional wealth as a mixed gamble: Revisiting family firm R&D investments with the behavioral agency model. *Entrepreneurship Theory and Practice, 38*(6), 1351–1374.

Gottardo, P., & Moisello, A. M. (2014). The capital structure choices of family firms. *Managerial Finance, 40*, 254–275.

Hauck, J., Suess-Reyes, J., Beck, S., Prügl, R., & Frank, H. (2016). Measuring socioemotional wealth in family-owned and-managed firms: A validation and short form of the FIBER scale. *Journal of Family Business Strategy, 7*(3), 133–148.

Haynes, G., Walker, R., Rowe, B., & Hong, G. (1999). The intermingling of business and family finances in family owned businesses. *Family Business Review, 12*, 225–239.

Hillier, D., Martínez, B., Patel, P. C., Pindado, J., & Requejo, I. (2018). Pound of flesh? Debt contract strictness and family firms. *Entrepreneurship Theory and Practice, 42*(2), 259–282.

Jaffe, D. T., & Lane, S. H. (2004). Sustaining a family dynasty: Key issues facing complex multigenerational business-and investment-owning families. *Family Business Review, 17*(1), 81–98.

King, M. R., & Santor, E. B. (2008). Family values: Ownership structure and performance of Canadian firms. *Journal of Banking & Finance, 32*, 2423–2432.

Koropp, C., Kellermanns, F. W., Grichnik, D., & Stanley, L. (2014). Financial decision making in family firms: An adaptation of the theory of planned behavior. *Family Business Review, 27*(4), 307–327.

Lardon, A., Deloof, M., & Jorissen, A. (2017). Outside CEOs, board control and the financing policy of small privately held family firms. *Journal of Family Business Strategy, 8*(1), 29–41.

Le Breton-Miller, I., & Miller, D. (2013). Socioemotional wealth across the family firm life cycle: A commentary on "Family business survival and the role of boards". *Entrepreneurship Theory and Practice, 37*, 1391–1397.

Le Breton-Miller, I., Miller, D., & Lester, R. H. (2011). Stewardship or agency? A social embeddedness reconciliation of conduct and performance in public family businesses. *Organization Science, 22*(3), 704–721.

Lehmann, E., & Neuberger, D. (2001). Do lending relationships matter? Evidence from bank survey data in Germany. *Journal of Economic Behavior & Organization, 45*, 339–359.

Lopez-Gracia, J., & Sanchez-Andujar, S. (2007). Financial structure of the family business: Evidence from a group of small Spanish firms. *Family Business Review, 20*, 269–287.

Ma, L., Ma, S., & Tian, G. (2017). Corporate opacity and cost of debt for family firms. *European Accounting Review, 26*(1), 27–59.

Mahérault, L. (2000). The influence of going public on investment policy: An empirical study of french family-owned businesses. *Family Business Review, 13*, 71–79.

Mahérault, L. (2004). Is there any specific equity route for small and medium-sized family businesses? The French experience. *Family Business Review, 17*(3), 221–235.

Margaritis, D., & Psillaki, M. (2010). Capital structure, equity ownership and firm performance. *Journal of Banking & Finance, 34*(3), 621–632.

Martin, G., Campbell, J. T., & Gómez-Mejía, L. R. (2016). Family control, socioemotional wealth and earnings management in publicly traded firms. *Journal of Business Ethics, 133*(3), 453–469.

McConaughy, D. L. (1999). Is the cost of capital different for family firms? *Family Business Review, 12*, 353–359.

McConaughy, D. L., & Phillips, G. M. (1999). Founders versus descendants: The profitability, efficiency, growth characteristics and financing in large, public, founding family-controlled firms. *Family Business Review, 12*, 123–132.

Mengoli, S., Pazzaglia, F., & Sapienza, E. (2009). Effect of governance reforms on corporate ownership in Italy: Is it still pizza, spaghetti, and mandolino? *Corporate Governance: An International Review, 17*, 629–645.

Michaelas, N., Chittenden, F., & Poutziouris, P. (1999). Financial policy and capital structure choice in U.K. SMEs: Empirical evidence from company panel data. *Small Business Economics, 12*, 113–130.

Michiels, A., & Molly, V. (2017). Financing decisions in family businesses: A review and suggestions for developing the field. *Family Business Review, 30*(4), 369–399.

Miller, D., & Le Breton-Miller, I. (2014). Deconstructing socioemotional wealth. *Entrepreneurship Theory and Practice, 38*(4), 713–720.

Miller, D., Le Breton-Miller, I., & Lester, R. H. (2013). Family firm governance, strategic conformity, and performance: Institutional vs. strategic perspectives. *Organization Science, 24*(1), 189–209.

Molly, V., Laveren, E., & Deloof, M. (2010). Family business succession and its impact on financial structure and performance. *Family Business Review, 23*, 131–147.

Molly, V., Laveren, E., & Jorissen, A. (2012). Intergenerational differences in family firms: Impact on capital structure and growth behavior. *Entrepreneurship Theory and Practice, 36*(4), 703–725.

Morck, R., Shleifer, A., & Vishny, R. W. (1988). Management ownership and market valuation. *Journal of Financial Economics, 20*, 293–315.

Myers, S. C., & Majluf, N. S. (1984). Corporate financing and investment decisions when firms have information that investors do not have. *Journal of Financial Economics, 13*, 187–221.

Naldi, L., Nordqvist, M., Sjöberg, K., & Wiklund, J. (2007). Entrepreneurial orientation, risk taking, and performance in family firms. *Family Business Review, 20*, 33–47.

Naldi, L., Cennamo, C., Corbetta, G., & Gómez-Mejía, L. R. (2013). Preserving socioemotional wealth in family firms: Asset or liability? The moderating role of business context. *Entrepreneurship Theory and Practice, 37*, 1341–1360.

Nishihara, M., & Shibata, T. (2014). Preemption, leverage, and financing constraints. *Review of Financial Economics, 23*, 75–89.
Petersen, M. A. (2009). Estimating standard errors in finance panel datasets: Comparing approaches. *Review of Financial Studies, 22*, 435–480.
Pindado, J., Requejo, I., & de la Torre, C. (2015). Does family control shape corporate capital structure? An empirical analysis of eurozone firms. *Journal of Business Finance & Accounting, 42*(7–8), 965–1006.
Poutziouris, P. Z. (2001). The views of family companies on Venture capital: Empirical evidence from the UK small to medium-size enterprising economy. *Family Business Review, 14*(3), 277–291.
Rajan, R. G., & Zingales, L. (1995). What do we know about capital structure? Some evidence from international data. *Journal of Finance, 50*, 1421–1460.
Ramalho, J. J., Rita, R. M., & da Silva, J. V. (2018). The impact of family ownership on capital structure of firms: Exploring the role of zero-leverage, size, location and the global financial crisis. *International Small Business Journal, 36*(5), 574–604.
Ravasi, D., & Marchisio, G. (2003). Going public and the enrichment of a supportive network. *Small Business Economics, 21*, 381–395.
Romano, C. A., Tanewsky, G. A., & Smyrnios, K. X. (2000). Capital structure decision making: A model for family business. *Journal of Business Venturing, 16*, 285–310.
Salvato, C., & Moores, K. (2010). Research on accounting in family firms: Past accomplishments and future challenges. *Family Business Review, 23*, 193–215.
Schmid, T. (2013). Control considerations, creditor monitoring, and the capital structure of family firms. *Journal of Banking & Finance, 37*(2), 257–272.
Schulze, W. S., Lubatkin, M. H., & Dino, R. N. (2003). Exploring the agency consequences of ownership dispersion among the directors of private family firms. *Academy of Management Journal, 46*, 179–194.
Setia-Atmaja, L., Tanewski, G., & Skully, M. (2009). The role of dividends, debt and board structure in the governance of family controlled firms. *Journal of Business Finance & Accounting, 36*, 863–898.
Sharma, P. (2004). An overview of the field of family business studies: Current status and directions for the future. *Family Business Review, 17*, 1–36.
Sharma, P., & Manikuti, S. (2005). Strategic divestments in family firms: Role of family structure and community culture. *Entrepreneurship Theory and Practice, 29*, 293–311.
Sirmon, D. G., & Hitt, M. A. (2003). Managing resources: Linking unique resources, management, and wealth creation in family firms. *Entrepreneurship Theory and Practice, 27*, 339–358.
Titman, S. (1984). The effect of capital structure on a firm's liquidation decision. *Journal of Financial Economics, 13*, 137–151.
Uhlaner, L. M., Kellermanns, F., Eddeleston, K., & Hoy, F. (2012). The entrepreneuring family: A new paradigm for family business research. *Small Business Economics, 38*, 1–11.
Villalonga, B., & Amit, R. (2010). Family control of firms and industries. *Financial Management, 39*, 863–904.
Voordeckers, W., Van Gils, A., & Van den Heuvel, J. (2007). Board composition in small and medium-sized family firms. *Journal of Small Business Management, 45*, 137–156.
Westhead, P. (2003). Company performance and objectives reported by first and multi-generation family companies: A research note. *Journal of Small Business and Enterprise Development, 10* (1), 93–105.
Westhead, P., & Cowling, M. (1998). Family firm research: The need for a methodological rethink. *Entrepreneurship Theory and Practice, 23*, 31–56.
Xi, J. M., Kraus, S., Filser, M., & Kellermanns, F. W. (2015). Mapping the field of family business research: Past trends and future directions. *International Entrepreneurship and Management Journal, 11*, 113–132.
Yen, J. F., Lin, C. Y., Chen, Y. S., & Huang, Y. C. (2015). Founding family firms and bank loan contracts. *Journal of Financial Services Research, 48*(1), 53–82.

Yilmazer, T., & Schrank, H. (2006). Financial intermingling in small family businesses. *Journal of Business Venturing, 21*(5), 726–751.

Zellweger, T. M. (2007). Time horizon, cost of equity capital, and generic investment strategies of firms. *Family Business Review, 20*, 1–15.

Zellweger, T. M., & Astrachan, J. H. (2008). On the emotional value of owning a firm. *Family Business Review, 21*, 347–363.

Zellweger, T. M., Kellermanns, F. W., Chrisman, J. J., & Chua, J. H. (2011). Family control and family firm valuation by family CEOs: The importance for intentions for transgenerational control. *Organization Science, 23*, 851–868.

Zellweger, T. M., Nason, R. S., Nordqvist, M., & Brush, C. G. (2013). Why do family firms strive for nonfinancial goals? An organizational identity perspective. *Entrepreneurship Theory and Practice, 37*(2), 229–248.

Chapter 3
Family Influence, Leverage and Probability of Financial Distress

Abstract This chapter studies leverage's effect on a firm's probability of financial distress taking into account different forms of family influence on the business. As family firms are a non-homogeneous group and their governance and management characteristics may impact on risk attitude and financial distress likelihood, we also take into account other measures of risk, board and CEO characteristics, accounting variables and macroeconomic indicators. We address this topic by analyzing a sample of 1137 Italian family and non-family private firms for the period 2004–2013, covering the pre and post financial crisis period. The findings point out that these variables have a different significance in family and non-family firms' probability of financial distress. Family firms have a lower probability of incurring in financial distress. Leverage has a strong effect for family and non-family firms, but a family's direct influence on the firm, by appointing a family CEO, has a significant lowering effect on a firm's probability of financial distress when a family exerts its influence directly.

Keywords Leverage · Family influence · Financial distress

3.1 Introduction

Literature suggests that family firms' system of corporate governance is a relevant source of competitive advantage (Carney 2005). Numerous studies addressed the issue of family firms' performance, and contrasting results emerge from the comparison between family and non-family businesses (Morck et al. 1988; Anderson and Reeb 2003; Vieira 2014). This evidence confirms that family companies are not a homogeneous group (Corbetta and Salvato 2004), they differ in relation to their generational stage, board characteristics and CEO type, so different conditions may affect their performance (Barontini and Caprio 2006; Villalonga and Amit 2006; Bennedsen and Nielsen 2010; Gottardo and Moisello 2015; Dyer 2018). Literature suggests that family companies are risk averse (Naldi et al. 2007;

P. Gottardo, A. M. Moisello, *Capital Structure, Earnings Management, and Risk of Financial Distress*, SpringerBriefs in Business,
https://doi.org/10.1007/978-3-030-00344-9_3

Huybrechts et al. 2013), as they behave in order to pass a healthy business to future generations and to renew, through succession, the bonds between the family and the business (Berrone et al. 2012). On the other hand, empirical studies show that family businesses are risk averse and risk willing at the same time, as they are prone to taking performance hazard when the family's control is at risk, in order to preserve the non-financial returns that family members obtain through the business (Gómez-Mejía et al. 2007). For the same reason they do not avoid financial risk and they tend to be more levered than non-family firms (Croci et al. 2011; Gottardo and Moisello 2014).

Wilson et al. (2013) have addressed the issue of family businesses' likelihood of failure by analyzing a large sample of UK companies for the period 2007–2010. They point out that family firms have a higher survival probability than non-family businesses. Thus, it is interesting to develop this rather unexplored topic, by analyzing how family firms leverage choices affect the probability of incurring in financial difficulties. Given the ubiquity of family businesses in economies around the world (Faccio and Lang 2002; Villalonga and Amit 2006) and their role in global GDP production and job creation, there is a need to study how the above-mentioned family firms' peculiarities affect their probability of financial distress, which could be a harbinger of a company's ultimate failure.

We address this topic by studying a sample of 1137 Italian private firms for the period 2004–2013 in order to include the pre- and post-financial crisis periods. We analyze family firms' financial distress likelihood taking into account certain board and CEO characteristics, different measures of risk, a set of accounting variables and a series of macroeconomic indicators. We find that family ownership control, and influence by the means of a family CEO, reduces a firm's probability to run into financial distress. However, the effect is reversed when numerous family members have a seat on the board. We argue that this reverse effect is due to the main reference point in family firms' behavior, i.e. the preservation of the affective returns that the family derives from the business.

This paper is grounded on the Socioemotional wealth (SEW) framework, one that relates to the non-financial returns a family obtains by exerting its control and influence on the business (Gómez-Mejía et al. 2007). In so doing, we contribute to Socioemotional wealth literature, providing empirical evidence of this perspective. Moreover, we contribute to financial accounting literature on financial distress probability by focusing on family firms.

The remainder of the paper is organized as follows: Sect. 3.2 introduces the theoretical background; Sect. 3.3 presents the data and research methodology; Sect. 3.4 provides the results and discussion and Sect. 3.5 concludes pointing out implications and challenges.

3.2 Theoretical Background and Hypothesis Development

The prediction of a company's financial distress status has been a challenging issue for financial accounting studies for decades. The pioneering studies of Beaver (1966), Altman (1968, 2000) and Altman et al. (1977) provide models based on accounting ratios in order to individuate which of a firm's characteristics would provide an effective alarm for financial distress. Recently literature has taken into account qualitative information related to board members' ownership and insider holding (Chen and Du 2009). There is evidence that corporate governance characteristics significantly affect a company's likelihood of incurring financial distress (Lee and Yeh 2004).

3.2.1 Sew and Risk Taking

According to the Socioemotional wealth perspective, family businesses' uniqueness resides in having nonfinancial, as well as financial, objectives i.e. the preservation of family members' affective endowment in the firm they own (Gómez-Mejía et al. 2007). It is based on the Behavioral Agency Model which claims that decision makers act in order to avoid losses (Wiseman and Gomez-Mejia 1998; Gómez-Mejía et al. 2000). SEW literature points out that family firms behave in order to preserve and increase the stock of affect-related value that the owning family derives from the business. Socioemotional wealth utility affects family owners' value perceptions and they subjectively evaluate their ownership stake in monetary terms, unlike a market valuation based only on financial information (Zellweger and Astrachan 2008).

There is evidence that the preservation of this value is the main reference point for family firms' strategies, management processes, risk-taking behavior (Gómez-Mejía et al. 2007, 2011; Casillas et al. 2018), diversification and financing decisions (Gómez-Mejía et al. 2010; Gottardo and Moisello 2014), proactive stakeholder engagement and environmental management (Cennamo et al. 2012; Berrone et al. 2010) and voluntary disclosure behavior (Gavana et al. 2016; Gavana et al. 2017a). Family firms must evaluate financial gains and losses, as well as potential socioemotional gains and losses (Gómez-Mejía et al. 2014). Given the salience of the owning family's affective endowment, family businesses might be "willing to be vulnerable to the possibility of financial loss" (Gómez-Mejía et al. 2010, p. 225). Conversely, recent studies have deeply analyzed the interplay of financial and non-financial goals in family firms, pointing out that the two rationalities are not necessarily in contrast (Boers et al. 2017). On the one hand the pursuit of a good reputation in order to enhance the SEW has a positive effect on financial performance, on the other hand a good performance has positive outcomes for the SEW (Gómez-Mejía et al. 2018).

According to SEW theoretical literature (Berrone et al. 2012; Gómez-Mejía et al. 2011), a family's affective endowments in the firm are related to five main dimensions: family control and influence; family members' identification with the firm; binding social ties; the emotional attachment of family members, dynastic succession. Family control itself provides emotional returns to family members and, through it, a family can protect the affective values it derives from the business in terms of influence, sense of identification, social ties, and renewal of family bonds to the business for succeeding generations (Gottardo and Moisello 2014). Therefore, the preservation of family control of the business is the main concern for family members because it is the means of exerting its influence on the firm and derive the related non-financial returns that meet family members' emotional needs (Berrone et al. 2012; Gómez-Mejía et al. 2010). The desire to maintain family control is the reference point in addressing business risk. Family firms address risk in order to avoid losses of socioemotional wealth and, in so doing, they are both risk willing and risk adverse. Gómez-Mejía et al. (2007), in their pioneer study, point out that family firms avoid entrepreneurial risk, because bankruptcy would result in the loss of the family's economic and non-economic stocks invested in the business. On the other hand, they are willing to bear performance risk—that in extreme consequences can lead to bankruptcy and definitive loss of SEW—in order to preserve family control as it is a key source of emotional returns for family members (Gomez Mejia et al. 2007). This apparent paradox is due to the fact that family decision-makers think that performance hazard is an endogenous risk that can be managed (Gómez-Mejía et al. 2007). Lins et al. (2013) find that, in the period 2008–2009, during the financial crisis, family firms cut investment more compared to non-family businesses, and these cuts are related to greater underperformance. Therefore, the authors argue that families behave in order to increase the likelihood that the firm they own, and family control on the business, survive the crisis, at the expense of outside shareholders. Families avoid financing decisions which may put at risk family control or dilute their control stakes and family's influence, so they are more prone to endure the risks related to debt financing than non-family businesses (Gottardo and Moisello 2014). Family influence may be indirectly exerted, by appointing the board, or directly by the means of a family CEO and/or the presence of family members on the board. A family CEO is a key mechanism for retaining control over the company's assets and activity (Chua et al. 1999) because, compared to a non-family CEO, this provides the family with more control over operations and decisions (Hall and Nordqvist 2008). There is evidence that family CEOs are less prone to bear entrepreneurial risk than professional CEOs, but that the latter tend to assume lower venturing risk as their tenure increases and they develop stronger links with the owning family (Huybrechts et al. 2013).

Family members see the business as an extension of the family as they feel a keen sense of identification with the company they own (Berrone et al. 2012) and they are aware that the way a firm behaves may affect the family image, therefore they act in order to protect the firm's reputation (Deephouse and Jaskiewicz 2013). A company's financial distress and risk of ultimate failure would damage the owning family's reputation. The sense of identification is stronger when a family directly exerts its influence on the business, by the means of a family CEO, (Gavana et al. 2017a), enhancing the concern for the firm's reputation and image (Dyer and Whetten 2006). Conversely, this sense of identification tends to decrease in a firm's later generational stages when different family branches are involved in the business and pursue different interests (Gómez-Mejía et al. 2011). Empirical literature suggests that a family-based organizational image positively affects a family business' ability to increase sales (Craig et al. 2008) and it positively contributes to a firm's performance (Zellweger et al. 2012). As a matter of fact, family firms' commitment to constructing a good reputation may result in the better development of partnerships (Arya and Salk 2006) and the capability to attract high-quality employees (Connelly et al. 2011).

3.2.2 Hypothesis Development

The bonds between a firm and its internal and external stakeholders constitute a unique form of social capital for family firms (Sirmon and Hitt 2003) and they are strongly committed to its preservation; in fact, there is evidence that family businesses are particularly concerned with social and environmental problems (Berrone et al. 2010; Cennamo et al. 2012). In response to their commitment to the community, family businesses receive loyalty and support from their stakeholders (Niehm et al. 2008). These close social ties on the one hand meet the family members' affective needs for belonging and also develop the family's influence in the local community at large, on the other hand these bonds benefit the business in term of the availability of "timely and trustworthy information critical for business operations", business opportunities and funding (Zellweger et al. 2012) and help the company cope with periods of crisis. Ownership concentration allows family members to exert a strong monitoring on agency problems which may harm lenders' interests, such as asset substitution behavior (Steijvers and Voordeckers 2009) and creditors may be more prone to reschedule credit maturities in case of trading difficulties (Wilson et al. 2013). D'Aurizio et al. (2015) find significant evidence that the contraction in credit for family firms was smaller than that for non-family firms during the 2007–2009 financial crisis. Consistently, empirical literature points out that during crisis periods the consequences of credit rationing on capital structure are less severe for family than for non-family companies (Crespí and Martín-Oliver 2015).

The preservation of the business for the future generations, i.e. the last dimension of socioemotional wealth, has a strong influence on a family firm's investment horizon as well as entrepreneurial risk aversion (Berrone et al. 2012; Gómez-Mejía et al. 2011). Dynastic succession is the means to preserve family control of the business and a family's visibility, reputation and influence on the community over time. Families manage the firm as a long-term investment (Chami 2001) and they avoid risky strategies in order to pass on a healthy business to future generations and perpetuate the business and family control over time (Sirmon and Hitt 2003). Moreover, the preservation of the family dynasty in the business implies the perpetuation of the family's values through business operations (Debicki et al. 2017) and, in turn, the presence of ethics norms reinforces the development of social capital (Sorenson et al. 2009) and of trusty relations with lenders. Family managers, because of their long-term orientation, are more interested in preserving the owning family's name and reputation rather than raising short-term performance by the means of earnings manipulations (Prencipe et al. 2011). There is evidence that family firms provide a higher quality accounting information than non-family companies (Cascino et al. 2010). Although they are less likely to disclose the governance practices, they are more prone to warn for bad news than non-family firms (Ali et al. 2007). Family businesses' earnings present greater informativeness and their transitory loss components are less persistent (Wang 2006). Family firms' disclosure behavior and the close relations with lenders result in lower agency costs of debt and more favorable financing conditions, especially for privately held firms (Ang 1992). There is empirical evidence that family firms benefit from lower cost of debt financing than non-family firms due to the relationships they develop with lenders across time and generations (Anderson et al. 2003). Hillier et al. (2018), analyzing USA listed firms, find that lenders impose less strict contracts on family than non-family companies, even more so when the former are characterized by higher asset tangibility.

On the other hand, family control may also have an increasing effect on agency cost of debt, particularly in small private family businesses, when parental altruism, combined with family ownership and management, results in hold up, risk shifting behavior and adverse selection in the labor market (Lubatkin et al. 2005). These problems might affect financial indicators, resulting in more stringent lending conditions—i.e. higher cost of debt or covenants requirement (Steijvers and Voordeckers 2009)—or in lower access to long-term credit than short-term credit. Family businesses avoid risky investments and present a parsimonious behavior in allocating the capital they collect from external lenders (Carney 2005). Family owners are more prone to provide personal collaterals to banks, and in so doing they are more likely to avoid behaviors that jeopardize a firm's repayment capacity (Steijvers et al. 2010). Family firms are expected to be more compliant with debt commitments than non-family businesses (Corbetta and Salvato 2004) and, consistently, there is evidence that, also in the private companies' sector, family businesses get better access to long term debt than non-family firms (Díaz-Díaz et al. 2016). All in all, literature suggests that family influence on the one hand facilitates debt financing management, also during periods of crisis, on the other hand it moderates entrepreneurial risk in capital allocation, therefore we expect family influence to moderate the effect of leverage on a firm likelihood of incurring financial distress.

H1 Family influence moderates the effect of leverage on the probability of financial distress

3.3 Data and Methods

We collected data from the Aida database (Bureau van Dijk) for the period 2004–2013 to examine the above issue and test the related research question. In order to be included, a firm needed to respect four conditions: availability of at least 4 years of data; sales over €40 million in at least 1 year; a non-financial ATECO code; be a private firm. The final sample comprises 1137 firms, 138 are the firms which, in the period analyzed, entered a financial distress procedure (restructuring, voluntary liquidation, insolvency or a composition with creditors). The dependent variable is a dummy that takes value one if in a given year, a firm is in distress. The literature is not unanimous about what constitutes a family firm (e.g. Chua et al. 1999) but we identify them using an ownership threshold, considering a firm to be a family business if a family holds more than 50% of its equity and defining consequently a binary variable (Family). We also consider two proxies to account for the degree of control and influence that families exert on the business, namely a dummy for the presence of a family CEO, and a measure of the number of family members as a fraction of those who sit on the board (MultiFboard). We chose to take into account board structure as Lee and Yeh (2004), that, studying a sample of Taiwanese companies characterized by concentrated ownership, provided evidence that the percentage of directors held by the controlling shareholder is positively related to the likelihood of financial distress in the following year.

Previous literature on the determinants of a firm's financial distress relies on liquidity, profitability leverage, solvency indicators (Altman 2000). So, from financial accounts, we extracted information on Interest coverage, Cash flow, duration of Receivables, Stock turnover, Current ratio and Leverage (Debt/Equity), as a measure of financial risk.

We take into account a firm's Size (natural log of Assets) because this measure has been also used as a proxy for a company's visibility; more visible firms attract attention from a broader community and this enhances family firms reputational concerns (Palma et al. 2017; Gavana et al. 2017b). We also control for differences in financial risk using the sector Beta, and, for the macroeconomic situation, taking into account the yearly changes in GDP (ΔGDP).

To verify the impact of family control and influence on the likelihood of ending up in financial distress, we estimate a panel logistic model using the availability of firm-specific time-varying covariates over multiple periods, covering the recent recession in 2007–2010.

A variety of quantitative prediction models for distress/bankruptcy have been proposed in literature. Beaver (1966) developed a dichotomous univariate t-test, while Altman (1968) applied multivariate discriminant analysis. One of major limitations of traditional models, as they are based on a dichotomous separation of failed and non-failed firms in two different populations, is that they suffer from a sharp difference in the goodness of fit in the modeling and forecasting periods. Traditional models present also other shortcomings failing to account for the panel characteristics of real data and for the influence of macroeconomics conditions. The approach of duration models is different as they assume the samples to be drawn from the same population, and they are more flexible to account for multi-period datasets and a mutable macroeconomic environment. We follow Shumway (2001) and Nam et al. (2008) estimating a duration independent model where the individual hazard rate for each firm is independent of a particular point in time. In this specification we assume that the baseline hazard rate is a constant term and the individual hazard rate, $h(t|x_{i,\ t})$, for firm i, is independent from the survival period and from any particular point of time. As Beck et al. (1998) showed, when the probabilities of failure are sufficiently small, the continuous proportional hazard model can be estimated using a multi-period logit model. In discrete time the multi-period logit model takes the form:

$$P(y_{i,t} = 1|x_{i,t}) = h(t|x_{i,t}) = \frac{1}{1 + e^{-x_{i,t}\beta}}$$

where the $x_{i,t}$ are the time-varying independent variables.

3.4 Results and Discussion

Table 3.1 and Fig. 3.1 present descriptive statistics for the subsamples of family and non-family firms, distinguishing firms in healthy condition and in financial distress.

In Table 3.2 we present the estimates of the panel logit model for the overall sample and for the family and non-family subsamples.

Our findings indicate that leverage has a significant positive effect on a firm's probability of financial distress. Leverage has the same effect for family firms, but our findings also suggest that when a family exerts its influence directly, by appointing a family CEO the effect of leverage is more than balanced by the interaction term between these two variables. Therefore H1 is confirmed when a family directly manages its business. When a firm is led by a family CEO the concern for the preservation of the socioemotional wealth is higher, the sense of identification between the family and the business is stronger and, in turn, the concern for the reputational drawbacks an owning family would suffer in case of financial distress or failure of the business, increases. The reputational concern strongly affects family firms behavior (Sharma and Manikutty 2005; Dyer and Whetten 2006) because a family would lose the financial and non-financial returns related to its social capital (Berrone et al. 2010), that is made up of reciprocal and trusting relationship with internal and external stakeholders (Arrègle et al. 2007). The sense of identification results in a strong engagement in the preservation of a

Table 3.1 Summary statistics of firm characteristics for family and non-family firms

	Family firms		Non-family firms	
	Healthy	In distress	Healthy	In distress
	Mean (Stdev)	Mean (Stdev)	Mean (Stdev)	Mean (Stdev)
Size	17.61 (2.52)	10.93 (1.04)	17.67 (2.61)	10.52 (1.31)
Leverage	1.04 (2.43)	2.20 (11.66)	0.90 (5.41)	3.10 (8.82)
Interest coverage	24.34 (51.19)	4.77 (19.53)	24.77 (51.04)	5.41 (17.94)
Cash flow	0.02 (0.27)	−0.16 (0.36)	0.00 (0.30)	−0.10 (1.63)
Receivables duration	88.88 (52.26)	114.20 (113.53)	86.71 (86.00)	125.49 (136.95)
Stock turnover	62.45 (48.70)	88.73 (74.81)	56.04 (61.17)	77.15 (82.99)
Current ratio	1.53 (0.86)	1.07 (0.56)	1.44 (0.80)	1.21 (0.98)
Beta family	0.77 (0.26)	0.80 (0.23)	0.85 (0.31)	0.87 (0.29)
CEO	0.70 (0.46)	0.82 (0.38)	–	–
Multi-board	0.51 (0.34)	0.71 (0.31)	–	–

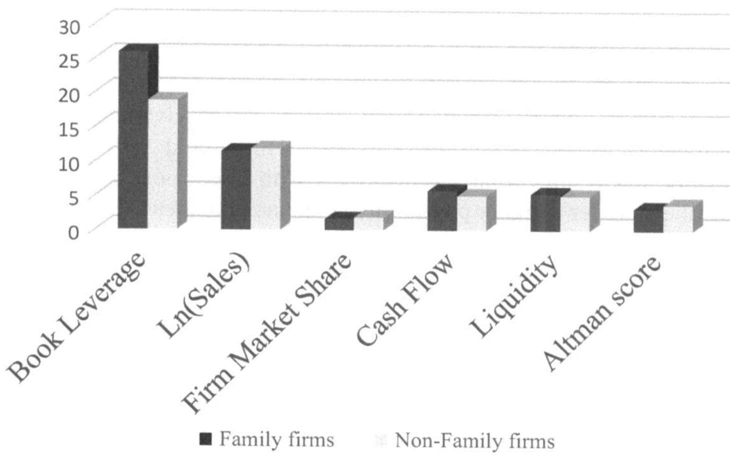

Fig. 3.1 Mean values: Family vs non-family firms

Table 3.2 Duration independent hazard model with time varying covariates. Period 2004–2013

	All firms	Family firms	Non-family firms
Intercept	13.87***	12.94***	18.02***
Independent variables			
Size	−1.25***	−1.19***	−1.64***
Leverage	0.07**	0.45***	0.12***
Interest coverage	−0.05***	−0.03***	−0.05***
Cash flow	−0.11	−0.12***	−0.13
Receivables duration	0.01***	0.01***	0.01***
Stock turnover	0.01***	0.01***	0.00**
Current ratio	−0.48***	−0.72***	−0.23
Beta	0.00	−0.33	0.44
ΔGDP	0.05	0.11*	−0.01
Family	−0.61***	–	–
Family CEO	−0.55**	−0.25	–
MultiFboard	1.92***	1.78***	–
Interactions			
*Leverage*FamilyCEO*		−0.48***	
Leverage*MultiFboard		0.00	
Log-Likelihood	−581.35	−344.47	−233.23
Wald-test	403.50	259.35	150.57
N (Obs.)	6032	3747	2438

***, **, * indicate significance at the 1%, 5% and 10% level respectively

company's image, also in the corporate debt market. International evidence suggests that family companies have a better reputation than non-family firms (Deephouse and Jaskiewicz 2013) therefore creditors have lower needs for monitoring and for strict debt contracts, which can cause a competitive disadvantage to a firm by imposing financial as well as non-financial costs (Hillier et al. 2018).

Conversely, our results point out that firms with larger boards, with numerous family members, suffer a higher probability of financial distress. This board characteristic is generally related to firms later generational stages (Westhead et al. 2002) in which the family members sitting on boards belong to different family branches and pursue the expectations and needs of their particular nuclear family. In later generational stages the sense of identification between the owning family and the business declines, the non-financial objectives are less relevant, and short-term earnings strategies can overpower the long-term survival goal (Gómez-Mejía et al. 2007, 2011; Le Breton-Miller and Miller 2013), putting the company's health at risk. These results are, therefore, consistent with the empirical studies of Arrondo-García et al. (2016) pointing out that, during the 2008 global crisis, family firms in different generational stages presented different attitudes towards financial risk.

Family firms, although more levered than their non-family counterparts, are more diligent and skilled at managing debt financing. This is probably due to the different role of debt financing in family and non-family firms and to family firms' debt maturity structure. Family firms are not prone to open their capital outside the family and they use debt financing in order to maintain family control over the business and preserve their socioemotional wealth (Gottardo and Moisello 2014). Debt contracts implies penalties and monitoring mechanism to restrict asset substitution and overinvestment. A covenant violation may involve the appointment of non-family members to the board or the passage of control rights to creditors (Hillier et al. 2018). Family firms are not prone to increase asset substitution or overinvestment because this behavior would put at risk the non-financial, as well as, the financial wealth of the owning family, that is mainly concentrated in the business. These motivations align creditors and families' goals in terms of compliance with debt contracts. As a matter of fact, family firms present a preference for long terms loans (Steijvers and Voordeckers 2016) as they imply fewer contract renegotiations, lower refinancing and bankruptcy risk compared to short-term debt (Ortiz-Molina and Penas 2008; Mishra and McConaughy 1999).

Families protect the control of the business as they view the firm as a long-term investment to be passed to future generations through dynastic succession (Berrone et al. 2010; Berrone et al. 2012) and, for the same reason they are risk adverse. Further, as our results suggest, they tend to invest in industries characterized by lower beta than non-family companies. The intention for trans-generational control, and long-term orientation, develops a strong relationship with both internal and external stakeholders and among those debt financiers who are more likely to be willing to grant credit facilities to family businesses. These connections also provide operational utilities to family firms in terms of customer acquisition (Arrègle et al. 2007) and the reduction of costs related to complex cooperative relationship management (Mohr and Puck 2013): consistently, we find that cash flow has a significant effect in lowering the financial distress probability only for family firms. On the contrary, the strong ties with customers may have a negative effect on the likelihood of survival when they result in excessive payment delays, as shown by the effect of credit duration on family firms' probability of financial distress.

Consistent with previous literature, we find that another firm characteristic, such as size, has a significant effect in lowering a company's probability of financial distress, but that the effect is lower for family firms. As a matter of fact, larger firms can rely on significant capital requirements barriers, which has a positive effect on performance (Hall and Weiss 1967). Size enhances a firm's visibility and the concern for financial distress impacts on a family's reputation (Gavana et al. 2016), but, at the same time, size is a socioemotional wealth moderator (Gómez-Mejía et al. 2011). As a firm grows a family may have to share its influence on the company with other parties, experiencing a lower sense of identification and deriving a lower emotional return from the business, which may result in opportunistic behavior and in a lower venturing risk aversion (Wasserman 2006).

Our results suggest that a family's influence on the business has a significant lowering effect on a firm's probability of financial distress. Our research, focused on a sample of firms operating in a bank-based economy, is consistent with the findings provided by Wilson et al. (2013) for a sample of companies operating in a market-based economy, providing evidence that the nature of family businesses has, ultimately, a strong influence on a firm's survival capability, regardless of the characteristics of the economy in which it operates. Moreover, our findings suggest that, overall, a firm's likelihood of financial distress is more significantly related to the nature of the ultimate controlling owner and its direct influence on the business, rather than to the economic situation of the country in which the company operates, in terms of changes in gross domestic product. This is consistent with the study of Johnson et al. (2000) that points out that governance characteristics are more significant than macroeconomic variables in the prediction of crisis. Family firms' lower probability of financial distress supports a recent contribution of Gómez-Mejía et al. (2018, p. 1373), which suggests that when a family company experiences a situation of vulnerability and financial duress, financial concerns and socioemotional wealth are "aligned as drivers of strategic change", as in this situation the achievement of a firm's financial obligations is the means, for the owning family, to preserve the affective endowment in the business and get financial utilities.

3.5 Implications and Challenges

This paper studies the effect of families' indirect and direct influence on a firm financial distress probability, analyzing a sample of 1137 Italian private firms for the period 2004–2013. Overall, our results suggest that a business' family nature benefits a company's survival likelihood regardless of the structural and conjunctural characteristic of the economy in which it operates. The beneficial effect of family influence is stronger when it is exerted by means of a family CEO as it implies a higher emotional return from the business for the family, which would decrease or fade away, respectively, in case of financial distress or bankruptcy. We find the opposite effect when family influence is explicated by the presence of numerous family members on large boards.

This paper addresses family firms' financial distress probability, focusing on the effect of family control and influence dimension. However, other SEW dimensions would also be of interest. It would be useful to broaden the analyses by taking into consideration, in the regression model, family ties with internal and external stakeholders. Moreover, given that the attitude to release company control varies from country to country (Franks et al. 2011), further research may usefully focus on a cross-national sample in order to better control for the effect of different institutional and cultural settings on a family firm's probability of financial distress.

References

Ali, A., Chen, T. Y., & Radhakrishnan, S. (2007). Corporate disclosures by family firms. *Journal of Accounting and Economics, 44*(1–2), 238–286.

Altman, E. I. (1968). Financial ratios, discriminant analysis and the prediction of corporate bankruptcy. *Journal of Finance, 23*(4), 589–609.

Altman, E. I. (2000). *Predicting financial distress of companies: Revisiting the Z-score and ZETA models* (pp. 9–12). Stern School of Business: New York University.

Altman, E. I., Haldeman, R. G., & Narayanan, P. (1977). ZETATM analysis a new model to identify bankruptcy risk of corporations. *Journal of Banking & Finance, 1*(1), 29–54.

Anderson, R. C., & Reeb, D. M. (2003). Founding-family ownership and firm performance: Evidence from the S&P 500. *Journal of Finance, 58*, 1301–1328.

Anderson, R. C., Mansi, S. A., & Reeb, D. M. (2003). Founding family ownership and the agency cost of debt. *Journal of Financial Economics, 68*(2), 263–285.

Ang, J. S. (1992). On the theory of finance for privately held firms. *Journal of Entrepreneurial Finance, 1*(3), 185–203.

Arrègle, J. L., Hitt, M. A., Sirmon, D. G., & Very, P. (2007). The development of organizational social capital: Attributes of family firms. *Journal of Management Studies, 44*(1), 73–95.

Arrondo-García, R., Fernández-Méndez, C., & Menéndez-Requejo, S. (2016). The growth and performance of family businesses during the global financial crisis: The role of the generation in control. *Journal of Family Business Strategy, 7*(4), 227–237.

Arya, B., & Salk, J. E. (2006). Cross-sector alliance learning and effectiveness of voluntary codes of corporate social responsibility. *Business Ethics Quarterly, 16*(02), 211–234.

Barontini, R., & Caprio, L. (2006). The effect of family control on firm value and performance: Evidence from continental Europe. *European Financial Management, 12*(5), 689–723.

Beaver, W. H. (1966). Financial ratios as predictors of failure. *Journal of Accounting Research, 4*, 71–111.

Beck, N., Katz, J. N., & Tucker, R. (1998). Taking time seriously: Time-series-cross-section analysis with a binary dependent variable. *American Journal of Political Science, 42*(4), 1260–1288.

Bennedsen, M., & Nielsen, K. M. (2010). Incentive and entrenchment effects in European ownership. *Journal of Banking & Finance, 34*(9), 2212–2229.

Berrone, P., Cruz, C., Gómez-Mejía, L. R., & Larraza-Kintana, M. (2010). Socioemotional wealth and corporate responses to institutional pressures: Do family-controlled firms pollute less? *Administrative Science Quarterly, 55*(1), 82–113.

Berrone, P., Cruz, C., & Gómez-Mejía, L. R. (2012). Socioemotional wealth in family firms: Theoretical dimensions, assessment approaches, and agenda for future research. *Family Business Review, 25*(3), 258–279.
Boers, B., Ljungkvist, T., Brunninge, O., & Nordqvist, M. (2017). Going private: A socioemotional wealth perspective on why family controlled companies decide to leave the stock-exchange. *Journal of Family Business Strategy, 8*(2), 74–86.
Carney, M. (2005). Corporate governance and competitive advantage in family-controlled firms. *Entrepreneurship Theory and Practice, 29*(3), 249–265.
Cascino, S., Pugliese, A., Mussolino, D., & Sansone, C. (2010). The influence of family ownership on the quality of accounting information. *Family Business Review, 23*(3), 246–265.
Casillas, J. C., Moreno-Menéndez, A. M., Barbero, J. L., & Clinton, E. (2018). Retrenchment Strategies and family involvement: The role of survival risk. *Family Business Review*, https://doi.org/10.1177/0894486518794605.
Cennamo, C., Berrone, P., Cruz, C., & Gomez-Mejia, L. R. (2012). Socioemotional wealth and proactive stakeholder engagement: Why family-controlled firms care more about their stakeholders. *Entrepreneurship Theory and Practice, 36*(6), 1153–1173.
Chami, M. R. (2001). *What is different about family businesses?* (No. 1–70). International Monetary Fund.
Chen, W. S., & Du, Y. K. (2009). Using neural networks and data mining techniques for the financial distress prediction model. *Expert Systems with Applications, 36*(2), 4075–4086.
Chua, J. H., Chrisman, J. J., & Sharma, P. (1999). Defining the family business by behavior. *Entrepreneurship Theory and Practice, 23*(4), 19–19.
Connelly, B. L., Certo, S. T., Ireland, R. D., & Reutzel, C. R. (2011). Signaling theory: A review and assessment. *Journal of Management, 37*(1), 39–67.
Corbetta, G., & Salvato, C. (2004). Self-serving or self-actualizing? Models of man and agency costs in different types of family firms: A commentary on "comparing the agency costs of family and non-family firms: Conceptual issues and exploratory evidence". *Entrepreneurship Theory and Practice, 28*(4), 355–362.
Craig, J. B., Dibrell, C., & Davis, P. S. (2008). Leveraging family-based brand identity to enhance firm competitiveness and performance in family businesses. *Journal of Small Business Management, 46*(3), 351–371.
Crespí, R., & Martín-Oliver, A. (2015). Do family firms have better access to external finance during crises? *Corporate Governance: An International Review, 23*(3), 249–265.
Croci, E., Doukas, J. A., & Gonenc, H. (2011). Family control and financing decisions. *European Financial Management, 17*(5), 860–897.
D'Aurizio, L., Oliviero, T., & Romano, L. (2015). Family firms, soft information and bank lending in a financial crisis. *Journal of Corporate Finance, 33*, 279–292.
Debicki, B. J., Van de Graaff Randolph, R., & Sobczak, M. (2017). Socioemotional wealth and family firm performance: A stakeholder approach. *Strategic Issues in the Family Firm, 29*(1), 82–111.
Deephouse, D. L., & Jaskiewicz, P. (2013). Do family firms have better reputations than non-family firms? An integration of socioemotional wealth and social identity theories. *Journal of Management Studies, 50*(3), 337–360.
Díaz-Díaz, N. L., García-Teruel, P. J., & Martínez-Solano, P. (2016). Debt maturity structure in private firms: Does the family control matter? *Journal of Corporate Finance, 37*, 393–411.
Dyer, W. G. (2018). Are family firms really better? Reexamining "Examining the 'Family Effect on Firm Performance". *Family Business Review, 31*(2), 240–248.
Dyer, W. G., & Whetten, D. A. (2006). Family firms and social responsibility: Preliminary evidence from the S&P 500. *Entrepreneurship Theory and Practice, 30*(6), 785–802.
Faccio, M., & Lang, L. H. (2002). The ultimate ownership of Western European corporations. *Journal of Financial Economics, 65*(3), 365–395.
Franks, J., Mayer, C., Volpin, P., & Wagner, H. F. (2011). The life cycle of family ownership: International evidence. *Review of Financial Studies, 25*(6), 1675–1712.

Gavana, G., Gottardo, P., & Moisello, A. M. (2016). Sustainability reporting in family firms: A panel data analysis. *Sustainability, 9*(1), 38.
Gavana, G., Gottardo, P., & Moisello, A. M. (2017a). The effect of equity and bond issues on sustainability disclosure. Family vs non-family Italian firms. *Social Responsibility Journal, 13* (1), 126–142.
Gavana, G., Gottardo, P., & Moisello, A. M. (2017b). Earnings management and CSR disclosure. Family vs. non-family firms. *Sustainability, 9*(12), 2327.
Gómez-Mejía, L. R., Welbourne, T. M., & Wiseman, R. M. (2000). The role of risk sharing and risk taking under gainsharing. *Academy of Management Review, 25*(3), 492–507.
Gómez-Mejía, L. R., Haynes, K. T., Núñez-Nickel, M., Jacobson, K. J., & Moyano-Fuentes, J. (2007). Socioemotional wealth and business risks in family-controlled firms: Evidence from Spanish olive oil mills. *Administrative Science Quarterly, 52*(1), 106–137.
Gómez-Mejía, L. R., Makri, M., & Kintana, M. L. (2010). Diversification decisions in family-controlled firms. *Journal of Management Studies, 47*(2), 223–252.
Gómez-Mejía, L. R., Cruz, C., Berrone, P., & De Castro, J. (2011). The bind that ties: Socioemotional wealth preservation in family firms. *Academy of Management Annals, 5*(1), 653–707.
Gómez-Mejía, L. R., Campbell, J. T., Martin, G., Hoskisson, R. E., Makri, M., & Sirmon, D. G. (2014). Socioemotional wealth as a mixed gamble: Revisiting family firm R & D investments with the behavioral agency model. *Entrepreneurship Theory and Practice, 38*(6), 1351–1374.
Gómez-Mejía, L. R., Patel, P. C., & Zellweger, T. M. (2018). In the horns of the dilemma: Socioemotional wealth, financial wealth, and acquisitions in family firms. *Journal of Management, 44*(4), 1369–1397.
Gottardo, P., & Moisello, A. M. (2014). The capital structure choices of family firms: Evidence from Italian medium-large unlisted firms. *Managerial Finance, 40*(3), 254–275.
Gottardo, P., & Moisello, A. M. (2015). The impact of socioemotional wealth on family firms' financial performance. *Problems and Perspectives in Management, 13*(1), 67–77.
Hall, A., & Nordqvist, M. (2008). Professional management in family businesses: Toward an extended understanding. *Family Business Review, 21*(1), 51–69.
Hall, M., & Weiss, L. (1967). Firm size and profitability. *Review of Economics and Statistics, 49*, 319–331.
Hillier, D., Martínez, B., Patel, P. C., Pindado, J., & Requejo, I. (2018). Pound of flesh? Debt contract strictness and family firms. *Entrepreneurship Theory and Practice, 42*(2), 259–282.
Huybrechts, J., Voordeckers, W., & Lybaert, N. (2013). Entrepreneurial risk taking of private family firms: The influence of a nonfamily CEO and the moderating effect of CEO tenure. *Family Business Review, 26*(2), 161–179.
Johnson, S., Boone, P., Breach, A., & Friedman, E. (2000). Corporate governance in the Asian financial crisis. *Journal of Financial Economics, 58*, 141–186.
Le Breton-Miller, I., & Miller, D. (2013). Socioemotional wealth across the family firm life cycle: A commentary on "Family Business Survival and the Role of Boards". *Entrepreneurship Theory and Practice, 37*(6), 1391–1397.
Lee, T. S., & Yeh, Y. H. (2004). Corporate governance and financial distress: Evidence from Taiwan. *Corporate Governance: An International Review, 12*(3), 378–388.
Lins, K. V., Volpin, P., & Wagner, H. F. (2013). Does family control matter? International evidence from the 2008–2009 financial crisis. *Review of Financial Studies, 26*(10), 2583–2619.
Lubatkin, M. H., Schulze, W. S., Ling, Y., & Dino, R. N. (2005). The effects of parental altruism on the governance of family-managed firms. *Journal of Organizational Behavior, 26*(3), 313–330.
Mishra, C. S., & McConaughy, D. L. (1999). Founding family control and capital structure: The risk of loss of control and the aversion to debt. *Entrepreneurship Theory and Practice, 23*(4), 53–53.
Mohr, A. T., & Puck, J. (2013). Revisiting the trust-performance link in strategic alliances. *Management International Review, 53*(2), 269–289.
Morck, R., Shleifer, A., & Vishny, R. W. (1988). Management ownership and market valuation: An empirical analysis. *Journal of Financial Economics, 20*, 293–315.

Naldi, L., Nordqvist, M., Sjöberg, K., & Wiklund, J. (2007). Entrepreneurial orientation, risk taking, and performance in family firms. *Family Business Review, 20*(1), 33–47.

Nam, C., Kim, T., Park, N., & Lee, H. (2008). Bankruptcy prediction using a discrete-time duration model incorporating temporal and macroeconomic dependencies. *Journal of Forecasting, 27*, 493–506.

Niehm, L. S., Swinney, J., & Miller, N. J. (2008). Community social responsibility and its consequences for family business performance. *Journal of Small Business Management, 46* (3), 331–350.

Ortiz-Molina, H., & Penas, M. F. (2008). Lending to small businesses: The role of loan maturity in addressing information problems. *Small Business Economics, 30*(4), 361–383.

Palma, M., Lourenço, I., & Branco, M. (2017, October). Sustainability reporting in family versus non-family firms: The role of the richest European families. In *Proceedings of the XVI Congresso Internacional de Contabilidade e Auditoria (XVI CICA)* (pp. 12–13). Aveiro, Portugal.

Prencipe, A., Bar-Yosef, S., Mazzola, P., & Pozza, L. (2011). Income smoothing in family-controlled companies: Evidence from Italy. *Corporate Governance: An International Review, 19*(6), 529–546.

Sharma, P., & Manikutty, S. (2005). Strategic divestments in family firms: Role of family structure and community culture. *Entrepreneurship Theory and Practice, 29*(3), 293–311.

Shumway, T. (2001). Forecasting bankruptcy more accurately: A simple hazard model. *Journal of Business, 74*, 101–124.

Sirmon, D. G., & Hitt, M. A. (2003). Managing resources: Linking unique resources, management, and wealth creation in family firms. *Entrepreneurship Theory and Practice, 27*(4), 339–358.

Sorenson, R. L., Goodpaster, K. E., Hedberg, P. R., & Yu, A. (2009). The family point of view, family social capital, and firm performance an exploratory test. *Family Business Review, 22*(3), 239–253.

Steijvers, T., & Voordeckers, W. (2009). Private family ownership and the agency costs of debt. *Family Business Review, 22*(4), 333–346.

Steijvers, T., & Voordeckers, W. (2016). Credit rationing in family firms: Short-term vs. long-term bank debt rationing. In *The Routledge companion to family business* (pp. 205–224). New York: Routledge.

Steijvers, T., Voordeckers, W., & Vanhoof, K. (2010). Collateral, relationship lending and family firms. *Small Business Economics, 34*(3), 243–259.

Vieira, F. E. S. (2014). The effect on the performance of listed family and non-family firms. *Managerial Finance, 40*(3), 234–253.

Villalonga, B., & Amit, R. (2006). How do family ownership, control and management affect firm value? *Journal of Financial Economics, 80*(2), 385–417.

Wang, D. (2006). Founding family ownership and earnings quality. *Journal of Accounting Research, 44*(3), 619–656.

Wasserman, N. (2006). Stewards, agents, and the founder discount: Executive compensation in new ventures. *Academy of Management Journal, 49*(5), 960–976.

Westhead, P., Howorth, C., & Cowling, M. (2002). Ownership and management issues in first generation and multi-generation family firms. *Entrepreneurship & Regional Development, 14* (3), 247–269.

Wilson, N., Wright, M., & Scholes, L. (2013). Family business survival and the role of boards. *Entrepreneurship Theory and Practice, 37*(6), 1369–1389.

Wiseman, R. M., & Gomez-Mejia, L. R. (1998). A behavioral agency model of managerial risk taking. *Academy of Management Review, 23*(1), 133–153.

Zellweger, T. M., & Astrachan, J. H. (2008). On the emotional value of owning a firm. *Family Business Review, 21*(4), 347–363.

Zellweger, T. M., Kellermanns, F. W., Eddleston, K. A., & Memili, E. (2012). Building a family firm image: How family firms capitalize on their family ties. *Journal of Family Business Strategy, 3*(4), 239–250.

Chapter 4
Equity and Bond Issues and Earnings Management Practices

Abstract Earnings management practices are potentially detrimental for stakeholders. Drawing on agency theory integrated with the socioemotional wealth framework we analyze firms' behavior around equity and bonds issues, comparing family and non-family firms' earnings management behavior. The data sample is represented by 226 non-financial listed firms for the period 2006–2015. We provide evidence that, in cases of equity emissions all firms significantly increase this practice, but family firms are less prone than their non-family counterparts to manage reported earnings. We do not find a significant effect in cases of bond issues. Our results suggest that the presence of the founder in management has an opposite effect on family compared to non-family firms' earnings management practices. In family firms, it significantly moderates this unethical behavior and the effect of the founder on earnings quality does not change in case of equity issues, while the effect is negative for non-family firms.

Keywords Earnings management · Family firms · Equity issue · Bond issue

4.1 Introduction

Literature has investigated earnings management practices by identifying the underlying motivations of this behavior. The principal motives refer to the achievement of contractual terms related to earnings, the will to influence the information used by third parties interested in a firm's performance, and, more specifically, by external investors (Walker 2013).

Research has investigated firms' earnings quality around IPOs and SEOs pointing out that firms tend to engage in earnings management in order to influence investors' information or to anticipate the effect of market behavior (Rangan 1998; Teoh et al. 1998a; Shivakumar 2000). There is also evidence of a relation between debt and earnings management as well as earnings manipulations and subsequent covenants

P. Gottardo, A. M. Moisello, *Capital Structure, Earnings Management, and Risk of Financial Distress*, SpringerBriefs in Business,
https://doi.org/10.1007/978-3-030-00344-9_4

violations (DeFond and Jiambalvo 1994; Iatridis and Kadorinis 2009). Literature has also addressed the issue of earnings quality in family firms by pointing out that these firms, in general, given their reputational concerns and lower agency conflicts, are less prone to engage in this unethical practice than non-family companies. To the best of our knowledge, no study has yet analyzed family firms' earnings quality around equity and bond issues. Earnings management (EM) practices may cause severe damage to stakeholders (Chi et al. 2015), mostly shareholders and lenders. Family businesses characterize the economies of the entire world, and in Italy, France and Germany they represent more than 60% of companies (Faccio and Lang 2002; Corbetta and Minichilli 2005), therefore it is of interest to study their earnings quality in relation to bond and equity issues.

We address this topic by drawing on Agency theory integrated with the Socioemotional wealth (SEW) construct as the preservation of the SEW shapes family firms' agency conflicts. We analyze earnings management practices, in terms of abnormal discretionary accruals reported in mandatory financial disclosures, of a sample of 226 Italian non-financial listed companies for the period 2006–2015. We take into account the presence of the founder, different forms of a firm's visibility, certain accounting variables, and equity and bond issues. We contribute to family firm literature as our findings indicate that, in cases of equity issue, family firms are prone to engage in earnings management although the effect is less significant than for non-family companies, particularly in the presence of the founder. We also contribute accounting literature as our results suggest that a firm's visibility affects earnings management and that the effect depends on the type of visibility and the nature of ownership.

The remainder of the chapter is organized as follows: Sect. 4.2 provides the literary review and develops the research hypotheses; Sect. 4.3 describes the methodology and data; Sect. 4.4 presents the results; Sect. 4.5 discusses the empirical findings and Sect. 4.6 concludes by pointing out implications and limitations of the present study and suggesting lines for future research.

4.2 Background and Hypothesis Development

4.2.1 Earnings Management, Equity and Debt

Literature on earnings management has focused significantly on the use of the accounting practice as a tool for managing share prices. Empirical findings show that seasoned public offerings (SEOs) anticipate poor earnings performance and lower stock returns, generating the suspicion that companies engage in earnings management, by means of abnormal positive accruals, in the period that precedes these events (Rangan 1998; Teoh et al. 1998a). There is evidence that issuing firms actively manage their earnings in the quarter in which they announce the offering and in the following quarter; earnings management around the period of the offering suggests earnings changes and adjusted stock returns in the subsequent year (Rangan

1998). Consistently, Teoh et al. (1998a) report the presence of earnings management activities for issuing firms, pointing out that the greater positive abnormal accruals the lower the subsequent earnings and stock returns. Shivakumar (2000) found evidence of earnings management practices around seasoned equity offerings but, in contrast with the above studies, he suggests that the stock market efficiently responds to inflated earnings, concluding that these practices are not used in order to mislead investors. The author suggests they are an answer to market reaction at issues announcements as investors, in such cases, assume that companies have inflated prior earnings and they discount its stock prices. Literature also shows that higher positive abnormal accruals anticipate shareholder lawsuits, and that a significant relation links the magnitude of the former with the settlement amount (DuCharme et al. 2004). Other studies show that, around SEOs, companies tend to use accruals-based earnings management together with real earnings management (Cohen and Zarowin 2010), as the latter is less likely to be detected by auditors and regulators (Graham et al. 2005). One piece of literature has investigated companies' behavior in terms of earnings management during initial public offerings (IPO). The pioneering study by Aharony et al. (1993) have investigated whether companies engage in earnings management in the periods before the year in which they become public, finding little, if any, manipulation through discretionary accruals. Their results also show that the cases of EM practices relate to small, high-levered firms. In contrast, Magnan and Cormier (1997) show that firms, during the first year as a public company, align reported earnings toward the forecasts disclosed at the time of initial offering. Teoh et al. (1998b) indicate that IPO firms, on average, tend to inflate earnings by abnormal positive discretionary accruals, leading investors to overpay for the IPO, and firms with the highest level of EM, as a result, experience the worst market performance. Consistently, Roosenboom et al. (2003) find, in a European setting, that firms manage their earnings in the first year after the IPO but not in the years before the IPO. They also highlight a negative relation between the magnitude of EM in the first year as a public company and market performance in the following 3 years. Conversely, Ball and Shivakumar (2008) find that initial public offering companies present more conservative reports because public firms have to face the higher quality reporting requested by investors and stronger monitoring and regulatory scrutiny. Other research suggests that EM may be used during an IPO for signaling purposes: Fan (2007) shows that ownership retention and EM are used in the context of high quality IPOs in order to signal a firm's confidence in the future and not to mislead investors who correctly interpret this signal.

Some studies have examined earnings management practices related to debt. Crabtree and Maher (2009) have studied the effect of EM on bond yield spreads, reporting a significant positive association. These results are consistent with the findings of Prevost et al. (2008) on the effect of EM on a firm's marginal cost of debt. In contrast, Liu et al. (2010) find that companies that inflate earnings in the year before new debt issues, by means of discretionary accruals, get a lower yield spread, coming to the conclusion that bond investors are unable to detect earnings management practices. In contrast, Ghosh and Moon (2010) have shown a non-linear relationship between debt and earnings quality, according to which debt first enhances earnings quality before the former reduces the latter. The authors suggest that, on the one hand, debt holders ask for higher-quality information and that this is why managers might use their accounting discretion to provide information in order to lower the cost of debt. On the other hand, in high debt contexts, firms would manage earnings to avoid covenants violations. There is also evidence that short-term debt is positively associated with earnings management and that a firm's creditworthiness has a moderating effect on this relation (Fung and Goodwin 2013). Jung et al. (2013) provide evidence that companies use EM in order to reduce earnings volatility and to alter ratings agencies' perception of credit risk, and in doing so, they are able to partially manage their credit ratings. Alissa et al. (2013) have addressed this issue by also taking into account real earnings management practices, coming to consistent results. Crabtree et al. (2014) have complemented this field of study by analyzing the effect of earnings management practices on the actual current rating assigned by analysts to new bond issues. Literature also provides evidence of a positive relation between debt covenant violations and earnings management, by means of accruals manipulation, in the 12 months preceding the year of the violation (DeFond and Jiambalvo 1994). Subsequent empirical literature confirms these results, suggesting that firms that are in capital need and are close to debt covenant violation are more prone to engage in earnings management practices (Iatridis and Kadorinis 2009).

4.2.2 *Earnings Management in Family Firms*

To the best of our knowledge, literature has not yet addressed the issue of earnings management practices around equity and debt emissions, comparing family and non-family firms' behavior. Nonetheless, research has provided interesting results on family firms' earnings management practices. A number of studies have addressed this issue, based on agency theory, which focuses the principal agent conflict, that is to say the conflict that emerges between owners and managers when the latter can pursue his/her self-interest because of information asymmetries (Berle and Means 1991; Jensen and Meckling 1976). Different agency conflicts characterize family and non-family firms as well as these problems differing between family firms themselves. Family firms present two different types of agency conflicts: between non-family management and the owning family and between family and non-family shareholders (Schulze et al. 2001; Le Breton-Miller et al. 2011). Family owners are motivated not only by financial objectives but also by strong non-financial goals (Gómez-Mejía et al. 2007) which moderate and shape family firms' agency costs (Chrisman et al. 2004). As a matter of fact, agency theory, as a standalone framework, cannot provide a full explanation of the differences between family and non-family companies or within family firms. These differences are effectively explained by the Socioemotional wealth framework (Gómez-Mejía et al. 2007; Gómez-Mejía et al. 2011; Berrone et al. 2012). This approach points out the complex stock of non-economic utilities, i.e. emotional values, family members derive from the business they own and the influence it exercises on a firm's behavior and its accounting choices as well (Ferramosca and Ghio 2018). These affective values derive from the family's control and influence on the firm and are related to the sense of identification between it and the company, to the social ties that the family develops through the business, to family members' emotional attachment, and to the "renewal of family bonds to the business" by means of dynastic succession (Berrone et al. 2012). Ownership control makes a family capable of exerting its influence on the business through a family CEO or, indirectly, by appointing the board members. Family control and influence are a source of emotional return in themselves and the means for preserving the other SEW dimensions. The desire to preserve these affective values affects family firms' corporate governance, their attitude towards risk, capital structure, value perception of their stakes, financial reporting, earnings management and voluntary disclosure extent (Gómez-Mejía et al. 2007; Zellweger and Dehlen 2012; Gómez-Mejía et al. 2014; Gottardo and Moisello 2014; Achleitner et al. 2014; Martin et al. 2016; Gavana et al. 2017a, b). Owing to their strong ties with the firm they own, families have a deep knowledge of the business. Therefore, on the one hand they suffer from lower information asymmetries between owners and managers but, on the other, given their concentrated ownership, they present a high level of monitoring capabilities. The presence of blockholders reduces first-type agency conflicts because large shareholders present strong incentives to engage in control activities, as the monitoring cost is lower than the returns on their stakes (Shleifer and Vishny 1986), and, for family firms, the return consists in both financial and non-financial benefits. Consequently, first-type agency costs are lower in family than in non-family firms (Anderson and Reeb 2003). The socioemotional wealth may affect second-type agency costs in opposite ways: families may be prone to assume performance risk in order to preserve their influence on the business (Gómez-Mejía et al. 2007), harming non-family shareholders' interests. They might also be less prone to monitor family members activity because of the emotional ties that bind them (Gómez-Mejía et al. 2011). On the other hand, the sense of identification between the family and the business, and the desire to pass on the business to future generations moderates behaviors which may damage a firm's reputation and durability.

4.2.3 Hypothesis Development

Literature provides mixed results on earnings management in family firms. Prencipe et al. (2008) do not find significant differences in family and non-family firms' earnings management practices as a means of avoiding debt covenants violations. Studying earnings management practices related to first-type agency conflicts, Ali et al. (2007) point out that family firms often have a family CEO, and/or family members on the board, and that their managers have low incentives to manipulate earnings. Wang (2006) finds a positive association between founding family ownership and earnings quality, which may be explained in terms of a better alignment of interests between the founding family and non-family shareholders and as compensation to non-family shareholders for the lower quality of family firms' corporate governance mechanism. Conversely, Yang (2010) provides evidence of a positive relation between earnings management and the level of family ownership, pointing out the presence of second-type agency costs. As a matter of fact, boards tend to be less independent in family than in non-family businesses and less effective monitoring may result in higher earnings management (Fan and Wong 2002; Chen et al. 2007). Moreover, there is evidence that board independence reduces earnings management practices, but that the effect is lower in family firms led by a family CEO and reversed in cases of CEO duality. This suggests that, in cases of direct family influence on the business, even independent directors act in order to satisfy the owning family's will (Prencipe and Bar-Yosef 2011; Cuadrado-Ballesteros et al. 2015). On the other hand, the literature indicates that firms owned by a founding family are less inclined to engage in earnings management practices than firms acquired by families. This is due to the fact that founding families have a strong sense of identification with the company and are concerned about its reputation (Pazzaglia et al. 2013). Consistently, Martin et al. (2016) indicate that family firms, in particular founder-led companies, are less prone to manipulate their earnings than non-family firms because of reputational concerns. Conversely, Stockmans et al. (2010) provide evidence that the influence of the founder may result in earnings manipulation if the threat exists that lenders may place covenants or non-family members on the board to monitoring their interests, to protect the SEW.

In general, the literature indicates that family firms are less prone to engage in earnings management, particularly when they are managed by the founding family and when they are in their earlier generational stages, that is when the founder exerts greater influence. Under these conditions, the different dimensions of SEW have a strong influence on a firm's behavior (Gómez-Mejía et al. 2011), suggesting that the protection of the affective endowments in the business exerts a moderating effect on earnings manipulation. Family firms are particularly worried that earnings management will be discovered and to mar the firm's image would cause a loss of SEW and negative financial consequences; this would be very dangerous for the family whose wealth is mainly invested in the company (Martin et al. 2016). Consistently, Martínez-Ferrero et al. (2016), studying the consequences of earnings management on a firm's reputation, point out a lower effect for family companies as they are less prone to engage in this unethical behavior. Moreover, in cases of equity emissions, earnings management practices result in subsequent conflicts with shareholders that may harm a firm's reputation, and the owning family's image given the sense of identification with the business.

H1 In cases of issue, family firms present a lower engagement in earnings management than non-family firms

More visible companies are under the lens of a broader public, they get more attention from stakeholders and are subject to a higher reputational risk. Therefore, they are more committed to preserving and presenting an ethical image (Morhardt 2010; Brammer and Pavelin 2006). Family managers are more interested in protecting a firm's reputation rather than in preserving performance by the means of earnings manipulations (Prencipe et al. 2011). There is evidence that family firms are more committed than their family counterparts to meeting stakeholders' expectations (Berrone et al. 2010). Empirical findings point out that the more visible firms are the more they engage in communicating that they act responsibly towards their stakeholders, and that this the effect is higher for family firms because they are concerned at being perceived as good citizens (Gavana et al. 2017a). Non-family shareholders are relevant stakeholders for family firms and we expect that the concerns for the consequences of unethical behavior, in terms of earnings management related to issues, is increased by visibility, and that this effect is stronger for family than non-family companies.

H2 The effect of a firm's visibility on earnings management is higher for family than for non-family companies

4.3 Methodology

The sample comprises the firms listed on the Italian Stock Exchange as of 2015 with the exclusion of banks, insurance companies and state-controlled firms, given their peculiar accounting and regulatory characteristics. Accounting data for the final sample of 226 firms, were gathered from the Aida (*Bureau van Dijk*) database for the period 2006–2015, while ownership and corporate governance data was hand collected using the Stock Exchange and Consob (*Commissione Nazionale per le Società e la Borsa*) websites as well as the Aida database. We define a firm as a family firm if the ultimate owner is a family that owns at least 20% of common shares (Villalonga and Amit 2010). To analyze the relationship between earnings management, issues and family status, we control for a number of variables, which may correlate with the quality of earnings: the presence of the founder, profitability, leverage, size, media exposure and industry (Dechow et al. 1995; Wang 2006; Park and Shin 2004; Prencipe and Bar-Yosef 2011; Stockmans et al. 2010; Kedia and Philippon 2009; McNichols and Stubben 2008; Paiva et al. 2018). The founder is a binary variable equal to 1 if he/she is still present on the firm's management. Profitability is measured by Roa. Leverage is given by the book value of the financial debt-to-equity ratio. We use three different measures of visibility: sales, total assets and media exposure. Firm size is a control variable for firm visibility, political costs, and media attention (Bhushan 1989; Watts and Zimmerman 1986). Media exposure is the number of articles including the firm's name that appeared in the Italian financial newspaper "Il Sole 24 Ore" for each year of the sample period. This is by far the most well-known daily source of financial information in Italy. Industry dummies control for sector differences in earnings management.

The dependent variable is absolute discretionary accruals estimated using the modified Jones model to assess earnings quality (Dechow et al. 1995; Bartov et al. 2000; Peasnell et al. 2000; Subramanyam 1996). This model separates the discretionary and non-discretionary components in total accruals, and the discretionary accruals can be used as a proxy for earnings quality.

Total accruals (TA) are defined as:

$$TA_{i,t} = \Delta CA_{i,t} - \Delta CASH_{i,t} - \Delta CL_{i,t} + \Delta STD_{i,t} - DEP_{i,t} \tag{4.1}$$

with:

$TA_{i,t}$ = total accruals
$\Delta CA_{i,t}$ = change in current assets in year t
$\Delta CASH_{i,t}$ = change in cash and cash equivalents in year t
$\Delta CL_{i,t}$ = change in current liabilities in year t
$\Delta STD_{i,t}$ = change in short-term debts included in current liabilities in year t
$DEP_{i,t}$ = depreciation and amortization expenses

Using a cross-sectional approach, we classify our sample firms by industry, retaining only the year-class with at least ten observations and estimate the following cross-sectional model for each year-class from 2007 to 2015, assuming that the independent variables represent the drivers of non-discretionary accruals, while the accruals which are not explained by the model are discretionary accruals.

$$\begin{aligned} TA_{i,t}/A_{i,t-1} = {} & \alpha_0 + \alpha_1(1/A_{i,t-1}) + \alpha_2[(\Delta REV_{i,t} - \Delta REC_{i,t})/A_{i,t-1}] \\ & + \alpha_3(PPE_{i,t}/A_{i,t-1}) + \varepsilon_{i,t} \end{aligned} \tag{4.2}$$

where:

$A_{i,t-1}$ = lagged total assets
$\Delta REV_{i,t}$ = change in revenues in year t
$\Delta REC_{i,t}$ = change in trade receivables in year t
$PPE_{i,t}$ = gross property, plant and equipment

The coefficients in Eq. (4.2) are then applied to estimate non-discretionary accruals for firm i in period t as:

$$\begin{aligned} NDA_{i,t}/A_{i,t-1} = {} & a_0 + a_1(1/A_{i,t-1}) + a_2[(\Delta REV_{i,t} - \Delta REC_{i,t})/A_{i,t-1}] \\ & + a_3(PPE_{i,t}/A_{i,t-1}) \end{aligned} \tag{4.3}$$

Finally, discretionary accruals (DA) for firm i in period t are calculated as the difference between total accruals and non-discretionary accruals:

$$DA_{i,t} = TA_{i,t}/A_{i,t-1} - NDA_{i,t}/A_{i,t-1} \tag{4.4}$$

4.4 Results

Table 4.1 presents descriptive statistics for the full and the subsamples of family and non-family firms (Figs. 4.1 and 4.2). Family firms exhibit absolute discretionary accruals that account for 7.5% of lagged total assets while, in non-family firms, they

Table 4.1 Descriptive statistics

Variable	All firms Mean (stdev)	Family Mean (stdev)	Non-Family Mean (stdev)	T statistics
Abs(Dis. Accruals)	0.084 (0.093)	0.075 (0.073)	0.090 (0.106)	4.61***
Equity issues	0.188	0.155	0.227	3.50***
Bond issues	0.026	0.025	0.058	0.19
Founder	0.459	0.530	0.297	−7.57***
ROA	−0.002 (0.111)	0.016 (0.083)	−0.016 (.124)	−7.19***
ΔROA	−0.004 (0.096)	−0.002 (0.062)	−0.005 (0.116)	−0.80
Leverage	1.29 (12.969)	1.48 (9.799)	0.994 (14.356)	−1.11
Total assets	12.382 (1.880)	12.710 (1.769)	12.59 (2.383)	−8.44***
Sales	11.517 (2.384)	12.08 (2.128)	11.51 (2.817)	−10.77***
Media exposure	9.548 (25.478)	11.319 (28.156)	8.288 (19.652)	−2.36**
Family CEO		0.612		
Family ownership		0.596 (0.151)		
Family on board		0.270		

***, ** indicate significance at the 1% and 5% level respectively

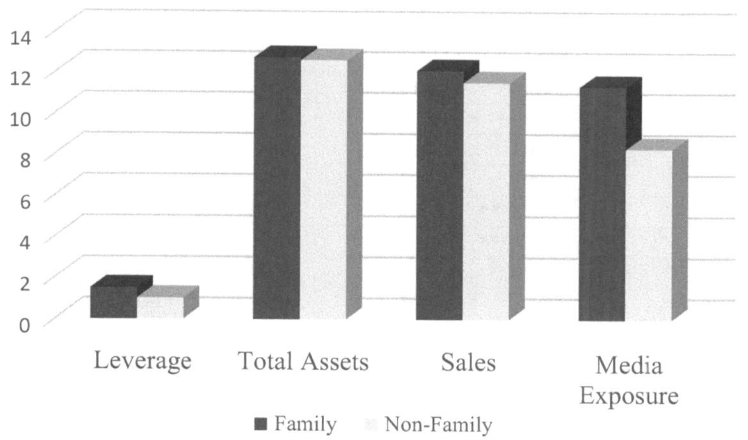

Fig. 4.1 Mean values: family vs non-family firms

represent, on average, 9% of assets. In the 2006–2015 sample period, we find that family firms resort less to external sources of funds issuing debt or equity. Firm profitability, measured by Roa, is higher for family firms (Chen et al. 2008) while the differences in leverage between family and non-family firms are negligible. More than 61% of family firms have a family CEO and the average ownership stake held by families is 59.6%. Family members represent, on average, 27% of the board in family firms.

Table 4.2 present the results of the regression models. To test our hypotheses, we run a pooling regression model with dummy variables to control for year and industry effects.

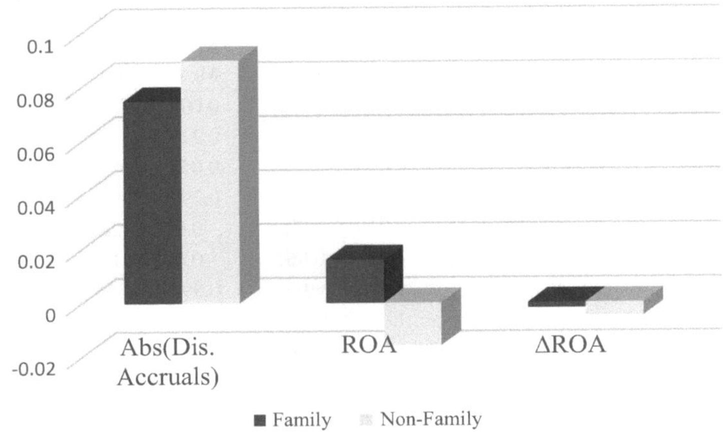

Fig. 4.2 Discretionary accruals and ROA (mean values): family vs non-family firms

Table 4.2 Pooling regression results

	All firms	All firms	Non-family	Family	Family
	Model 1	Model 2	Model 1	Model 1	Model 3
Int.	.146***	0.141***	.096**	.202***	.210***
Equity issues	.019***	.020**	.023**	.015**	.016
Bond issues	−.004	.013	.008	−.009	−.012
Founder	−.001	.007	.018*	−.011**	−.009*
ROA_{t-1}	−.078***	−.075***	−.110***	.012	−.015
ΔROA_{t-1}	−.001***	−.001***	−.061*	−.132***	−.129***
Leverage	−.000	−.000	−.000	−.000	−.000
Total assets	.001	.001	.008**	−.004	−.004*
Sales	−.007***	−.007***	−.010***	−.008***	−.008***
Media exposure	.000**	.000**	.000	.000***	.000***
Industry	Yes	Yes	Yes	Yes	Yes
Year	Yes	Yes	Yes	Yes	Yes
Family	−.003	.005			
qFam					.000
FBoard					−.022
Family*founder		−.015			
Family*equity issues		−.009			
Family*bond issues		−.026			
Founder*equity issues		.008			−.005
Founder*bond issues		−.003			.003
R^2	0.09	0.10	0.12	0.11	0.11
Obs.	1501	1501	650	861	831

***, **, * indicate significance at the 1%, 5% and 10% level respectively

The dependent variable in all models is represented by absolute discretionary accruals. H1 suggests that family firms, when the founder is still present in management, engage less in earnings management than non-family firms when they are involved in equity issuances. The results show that the founder has a positive and significant effect on earnings quality in family firms and a negative and significant effect in non-family firms. Taking into account the interaction effect of the founder and equity issues, we find that, for family firms, the issuance of new equity no longer has a negative impact on earnings quality, while this is still true for non-family firms.

H2 predicts that the impact of a firm's visibility on earnings management is higher for family than for non-family firms. The evidence here is mixed and related to the specific measure of visibility involved. The results show that total assets have a negative impact on earnings quality in non-family firms and, on the contrary, the effect is positive, albeit weakly significant, for family firms. Sales has a strong positive effect on earnings quality for both family and non-family firms. As Table 4.2 suggests, visibility in the financial press (media exposure) has a negative significant effect on earnings quality for family firms only.

4.5 Discussion

Family firms' behavior is guided not only by financial objectives but is strongly affected by the desire to preserve family members' affective endowments in the business (Gómez-Mejía et al. 2011). Consistent with H1, our results point out that family firms are less prone than their non-family counterparts to manipulate earnings, even when they are planning to engage in new equity issues. This is because they do not want to reduce or lose the non-financial returns that the owning family derives from the business. Earnings management practices, if detected, may affect the different SEW dimensions. The company is perceived as an extension of the family (Berrone et al. 2012), it is a mirror image of the family and a firm's unethical behavior could be seriously detrimental to the family name. Family firms' managers, given the reputational concerns and long durations of their roles, are more interested in preserving a company ethical image rather than in increasing short term financial performance (Prencipe et al. 2011). Moreover, they can count on deep bonds of trust with the owning family and they are aware of not risking their jobs in periods of poor performance (Ferramosca and Allegrini 2018). Earnings management practices may harm the social ties the family has built through the business as they put at risk stakeholders' trust, especially if they generate shareholder lawsuits. Family firms are known to be particularly careful regarding their internal stakeholders. Non-family employees form part of a sort of extended family; the negative financial consequences related to earnings management detection could cause some employees to leave and interfere with the family's emotional return from these bonds. The consequences could also jeopardize a family's capability to pass on a healthy company to future generations and to renew, by succession, its ties to the business. Given the strong reputational concerns, family firms are committed to preventing damage to their stakeholders (Deephouse and Jaskiewicz 2013; Dyer and Whetten 2006), among them lenders and shareholders. Our results suggest that the presence of the founder has a significant moderating influence on earnings management because he/she enhances the sense of identification between the family and the business and the desire to preserve the company for future generations. The effect of the founder on earnings quality does not change in case of issues.

The reputational concerns grow in correspondence with a firm's visibility as more visible firms suffer from potentially higher image damage, and, in accordance with H2, our findings suggest that, overall, visibility has a moderating effect on family firms' earnings management practices and that this effect does not change when bonds or equities are issued. Nevertheless, our findings suggest that a firm may present different forms of visibility which affect earnings management engagement in a variety of ways. Different forms of visibility imply visibility towards different types of stakeholders. In turn, these are likely to affect a firm's reputational concerns in varied ways. Sales indicates a firm's visibility for customers and it has a strong moderating effect both for family and non-family companies. Firms with high total assets have a strong impact on the environment and society; our findings underline that this form of visibility has a strong significant positive effect for non-family firms' EM, whilst the effect is negative for family businesses. These results suggest that family businesses suffer from greater concerns about the image they project in society than their non-family counterparts. Non-family companies' lower concerns allow them to exploit the size of their assets to manipulate earnings. Conversely, a firm's visibility by means of articles in the financial press, has a significant positive effect for family firms. This result is likely to be due to a sort of trade-off evaluation between the benefits and costs related to earnings manipulation. On the one hand, the cost is related to the reputational damage arising from a great visibility in the financial press, whose audience is mainly made up of financial investors. On the other hand, the benefit is related to the media resonance that an inflated performance may have if earnings management is not detected. All in all, these findings suggest that family firms' reputational concerns, and related effects on earnings quality, also differ according to the stakeholders to which the company is most visible.

The protection of SEW takes a number of forms and the preservation of family control and influence is key. There is empirical evidence that family firms shape their capital structure in order to avoid the dilution of the owning family stake and that they tend to be more levered than their non-family counterparts (Gottardo and Moisello 2014). In case of equity issues, in Italy shareholders have the right to underwrite a number of new shares so as to keep their equity stakes unchanged. As a firm engages in a new equity issue, the owning family has the tools to avoid a dilution of ownership control; the placement of the new shares is very important both from a financial and a reputational point of view. In accordance with the literature, they prevent the negative effects of investors' behavior, which, assuming that an offering firm has inflated earnings, tend to discount stock prices (Shivakumar 2000). For this reason, family companies, in the case of new emissions, tend to manipulate their earnings just like non-family firms do, but the effect is lower for family business for the reasons discussed above.

Conversely, we do not find a significant relation between earnings management and bond emissions both for family and non-family firms. These findings are consistent with literature, which points out that debtholders ask for high-quality disclosure (Ghosh and Moon 2010) and that a low earnings quality increases the cost of debt (Crabtree and Maher 2009), thus moderating a firm's earnings management practices. Literature, in analyzing the relation between leverage and EM, suggests that earnings manipulation is used in order to prevent debt covenants or the appointment by lenders of external members to the board (Stockmans et al. 2010; Prencipe et al. 2008) but that this motivation does not affect earnings quality when a firm is issuing new bonds.

4.6 Implications, Limitations and Suggestions for Further Studies

This chapter analyzes family and non-family firms' earnings management practices in relation to equity and bonds emissions, focusing on a sample of 226 Italian listed companies for the period 2006–2015. The results highlight that bond emissions do not affect earnings quality. However, in case of equity issues, family firms engage in earnings managment but the effect is lower than for their non-family counterparts. The effect is less significant for family firms given their concern for the preservation of the owning family's endowment in the firm which would be seriously damaged if EM were detected. All in all, our results indicate that a firm's visibility moderates earnings management practices but that the effect differs in relation to the type of visibility and to the firm's family or non-family status. Our findings suggest that visibility in terms of media exposure enhances EM. The effect is likely to be due to the type of media exposure taken into consideration in this study, i.e. financial press exposure. This enhances the potential reputational cost but, at the same time, increases the benefit related to inflated earnings. It would be of interest to also take into consideration different types of media exposure such as non-financial newspapers. Our results are of interest to investors given the potential detrimental effect of earnings management on their investment performance. This study has some limitations. The first is that our exploratory research focuses on the differences between family and non-family firms, taking into consideration the presence, or absence, of the founder. Further research should provide a more detailed analysis of family firms, examining board and CEO characteristics, as well as generational stage, in order to explore family firms' heterogeneity. The second limitation is that our analysis is single-country focused and it might be of interest to take into account the effect of different institutional and cultural aspects through an international sample.

References

Achleitner, A. K., Günther, N., Kaserer, C., & Siciliano, G. (2014). Real earnings management and accrual-based earnings management in family firms. *European Accounting Review, 23*(3), 431–461.

Aharony, J., Lin, C. J., & Loeb, M. P. (1993). Initial public offerings, accounting choices, and earnings management. *Contemporary Accounting Research, 10*(1), 61–81.

Ali, A., Chen, T. Y., & Radhakrishnan, S. (2007). Corporate disclosures by family firms. *Journal of Accounting and Economics, 44*(1–2), 238–286.

Alissa, W., Bonsall IV, S. B., Koharki, K., & Penn Jr., M. W. (2013). Firms' use of accounting discretion to influence their credit ratings. *Journal of Accounting and Economics, 55*(2–3), 129–147.

Anderson, R. C., & Reeb, D. M. (2003). Founding-family ownership, corporate diversification, and firm leverage. *Journal of Law and Economics, 46*(2), 653–684.

Ball, R., & Shivakumar, L. (2008). Earnings quality at initial public offerings. *Journal of Accounting and Economics, 45*(2), 324–349.

Bartov, E., Gul, F. A., & Tsui, J. S. (2000). Discretionary-accruals models and audit qualifications. *Journal of Accounting and Economics, 30*(3), 421–452.

Berle, A. A., & Means, G. G. C. (1991). *The modern corporation and private property*. New Brunswick, NJ: Transaction Publishers.

Berrone, P., Cruz, C., Gómez-Mejía, L. R., & Larraza-Kintana, M. (2010). Socioemotional wealth and corporate responses to institutional pressures: Do family-controlled firms pollute less? *Administrative Science Quarterly, 55*(1), 82–113.

Berrone, P., Cruz, C., & Gómez-Mejía, L. R. (2012). Socioemotional wealth in family firms: Theoretical dimensions, assessment approaches, and agenda for future research. *Family Business Review, 25*(3), 258–279.

Bhushan, R. (1989). Firm characteristics and analyst following. *Journal of Accounting and Economics, 11*, 255–274.

Brammer, S. J., & Pavelin, S. (2006). Corporate reputation and social performance: The importance of fit. *Journal of Management Studies, 43*(3), 435–455.

Chen, K. Y., Elder, R. J., & Hsieh, Y. M. (2007). Corporate governance and earnings management: The implications of corporate governance best-practice principles for Taiwanese listed companies. *Journal of Contemporary Accounting and Economics, 3*(2), 73–105.

Chen, S., Chen, X., & Cheng, Q. (2008). Do family firms provide more or less voluntary disclosure? *Journal of Accounting Research, 46*, 499–536.

Chi, C. W., Hung, K., Cheng, H. W., & Lieu, P. T. (2015). Family firms and earnings management in Taiwan: Influence of corporate governance. *International Review of Economics and Finance, 36*, 88–98.

Chrisman, J. J., Chua, J. H., & Litz, R. A. (2004). Comparing the agency costs of family and non-family firms: Conceptual issues and exploratory evidence. *Entrepreneurship Theory and Practice, 28*(4), 335–354.

Cohen, D. A., & Zarowin, P. (2010). Accrual-based and real earnings management activities around seasoned equity offerings. *Journal of Accounting and Economics, 50*(1), 2–19.

Corbetta, G., & Minichilli, A. (2005). Il Governo delle Imprese Italiane Quotate a Controllo Familiare: i Risultati di una Ricerca Esplorativa. *Economia and Management, 6*, 59–77.

Crabtree, A., & Maher, J. J. (2009). The influence of differences in taxable income and book income on the bond credit market. *Journal of the American Taxation Association, 31*(1), 75–99.

Crabtree, A., Maher, J. J., & Wan, H. (2014). New debt issues and earnings management. *Advances in Accounting, 30*(1), 116–127.

Cuadrado-Ballesteros, B., Rodríguez-Ariza, L., & García-Sánchez, I. M. (2015). The role of independent directors at family firms in relation to corporate social responsibility disclosures. *International Business Review, 24*(5), 890–901.

Dechow, P. M., Sloan, R. G., & Sweeney, A. P. (1995). Detecting earnings management. *Accounting Review, 70*, 193–225.

Deephouse, D. L., & Jaskiewicz, P. (2013). Do family firms have better reputations than non-family firms? An integration of socioemotional wealth and social identity theories. *Journal of Management Studies, 50*(3), 337–360.

Defond, M. L., & Jiambalvo, J. (1994). Debt covenant violation and manipulation of accruals. *Journal of Accounting and Economics, 17*(1), 145–176.

DuCharme, L. L., Malatesta, P. H., & Sefcik, S. E. (2004). Earnings management, stock issues, and shareholder lawsuits. *Journal of Financial Economics, 71*(1), 27–49.

Dyer, W. G., & Whetten, D. A. (2006). Family firms and social responsibility: Preliminary evidence from the S&P 500. *Entrepreneurship Theory and Practice, 30*(6), 785–802.

Faccio, M., & Lang, L. H. (2002). The ultimate ownership of western European corporations. *Journal of Financial Economics, 65*(3), 365–395.

Fan, Q. (2007). Earnings management and ownership retention for initial public offering firms: Theory and evidence. *Accounting Review, 82*(1), 27–64.

Fan, J. P., & Wong, T. J. (2002). Corporate ownership structure and the informativeness of accounting earnings in East Asia. *Journal of Accounting and Economics, 33*(3), 401–425.

Ferramosca, S., & Allegrini, M. (2018). The complex role of family involvement in earnings management. *Journal of Family Business Strategy, 9*(2), 128–141.

Ferramosca, S., & Ghio, A. (2018). Earnings Management in Family Firms. In *Accounting choices in family firms* (pp. 103–138). Cham: Springer.

Fung, S. Y., & Goodwin, J. (2013). Short-term debt maturity, monitoring and accruals-based earnings management. *Journal of Contemporary Accounting and Economics, 9*(1), 67–82.

Gavana, G., Gottardo, P., & Moisello, A. M. (2017a). Sustainability reporting in family firms: A panel data analysis. *Sustainability, 9*(1), 38.

Gavana, G., Gottardo, P., & Moisello, A. M. (2017b). Earnings management and CSR disclosure. Family vs. non-family firms. *Sustainability, 9*(12), 2327.

Ghosh, A. A., & Moon, D. (2010). Corporate debt financing and earnings quality. *Journal of Business Finance and Accounting, 37*(5–6), 538–559.

Gómez-Mejía, L. R., Haynes, K. T., Núñez-Nickel, M., Jacobson, K. J., & Moyano-Fuentes, J. (2007). Socioemotional wealth and business risks in family-controlled firms: Evidence from Spanish olive oil mills. *Administrative Science Quarterly, 52*(1), 106–137.

Gómez-Mejía, L. R., Cruz, C., Berrone, P., & De Castro, J. (2011). The bind that ties: Socioemotional wealth preservation in family firms. *Academy of Management Annals, 5*(1), 653–707.

Gómez-Mejía, L. R., Cruz, C., & Imperatore, C. (2014). Financial reporting and the protection of socioemotional wealth in family-controlled firms. *European Accounting Review, 23*(3), 387–402.

Gottardo, P., & Moisello, A. M. (2014). The capital structure choices of family firms: Evidence from Italian medium-large unlisted firms. *Managerial Finance, 40*(3), 254–275.

Graham, J. R., Harvey, C. R., & Rajgopal, S. (2005). The economic implications of corporate financial reporting. *Journal of Accounting and Economics, 40*(1), 3–73.

Iatridis, G., & Kadorinis, G. (2009). Earnings management and firm financial motives: A financial investigation of UK listed firms. *International Review of Financial Analysis, 18*(4), 164–173.

Jensen, M. C., & Meckling, W. H. (1976). Theory of the firm: Managerial behavior, agency costs and ownership structure. *Journal of Financial Economics, 3*(4), 305–360.

Jung, B., Soderstrom, N., & Yang, Y. S. (2013). Earnings smoothing activities of firms to manage credit ratings. *Contemporary Accounting Research, 30*(2), 645–676.

Kedia, S., & Philippon, T. (2009). The economics of fraudulent accounting. *Review of Financial Studies, 22*, 2169–2199.

Le Breton-Miller, I., Miller, D., & Lester, R. H. (2011). Stewardship or agency? A social embeddedness reconciliation of conduct and performance in public family businesses. *Organization Science, 22*, 704–721.

Liu, Y., Ning, Y., & Davidson III, W. N. (2010). Earnings management surrounding new debt issues. *Financial Review, 45*(3), 659–681.

Magnan, M., & Cormier, D. (1997). The impact of forward-looking financial data in IPOs on the quality of financial reporting. *Journal of Financial Statement Analysis, 3*(2), 6–17.

Martin, G., Campbell, J. T., & Gómez-Mejía, L. R. (2016). Family control, socioemotional wealth and earnings management in publicly traded firms. *Journal of Business Ethics, 133*(3), 453–469.

Martínez-Ferrero, J., Rodríguez-Ariza, L., & Bermejo-Sánchez, M. (2016). Consequences of earnings management for corporate reputation. Evidence from family firms. *Accounting Research Journal, 29*(4), 457–474.

McNichols, M., & Stubben, S. (2008). Does earnings management affect firms' investment decisions? *Accounting Review, 83*, 1571–1603.

Morhardt, J. E. (2010). Corporate social responsibility and sustainability reporting on the internet. *Business Strategy and the Environment, 19*(7), 436–452.

Paiva, I. S., Lourenço, I. C., & Dias Curto, J. (2018). Earnings management in family versus non-family firms: The influence of analyst coverage. *Spanish Journal of Finance and Accounting/ Revista Española de Financiación y Contabilidad*, 1–21.

Park, Y. W., & Shin, H. H. (2004). Board composition and earnings management in Canada. *Journal of Corporate Finance, 10*, 431–457.

Pazzaglia, F., Mengoli, S., & Sapienza, E. (2013). Earnings quality in acquired and non-acquired family firms: A socioemotional wealth perspective. *Family Business Review, 26*(4), 374–386.

Peasnell, K. V., Pope, P. F., & Young, S. (2000). Detecting earnings management using cross-sectional abnormal accruals models. *Accounting and Business Research, 30*(4), 313–326.

Prencipe, A., & Bar-Yosef, S. (2011). Corporate governance and earnings management in family-controlled companies. *Journal of Accounting, Auditing and Finance, 26*(2), 199–227.

Prencipe, A., Markarian, G., & Pozza, L. (2008). Earnings management in family firms: Evidence from R&D cost capitalization in Italy. *Family Business Review, 21*(1), 71–88.

Prencipe, A., Bar-Yosef, S., Mazzola, P., & Pozza, L. (2011). Income smoothing in family-controlled companies: Evidence from Italy. *Corporate Governance: An International Review, 19*(6), 529–546.

Prevost, A. K., Rao, R. P., & Skousen, C. J. (2008). *Earnings management and the cost of debt.* Available at SSRN. https://doi.org/10.2139/ssrn.1083808

Rangan, S. (1998). Earnings management and the performance of seasoned equity offerings. *Journal of Financial Economics, 50*(1), 101–122.

Roosenboom, P., van der Goot, T., & Mertens, G. (2003). Earnings management and initial public offerings: Evidence from the Netherlands. *International Journal of Accounting, 38*(3), 243–266.

Schulze, W. S., Lubatkin, M. H., Dino, R. N., & Buchholtz, A. K. (2001). Agency relationship in family firms, theory and evidence. *Organization Science, 12*, 99–116.

Shivakumar, L. (2000). Do firms mislead investors by overstating earnings before seasoned equity offerings? *Journal of Accounting and Economics, 29*(3), 339–371.

Shleifer, A., & Vishny, R. W. (1986). Large shareholders and corporate control. *Journal of Political Economy, 94*(3, Part 1), 461–488.

Stockmans, A., Lybaert, N., & Voordeckers, W. (2010). Socioemotional wealth and earnings management in private family firms. *Family Business Review, 23*(3), 280–294.

Subramanyam, K. R. (1996). The pricing of discretionary accruals. *Journal of Accounting and Economics, 22*, 249–281.

Teoh, S. H., Welch, I., & Wong, T. J. (1998a). Earnings management and the underperformance of seasoned equity offerings. *Journal of Financial Economics, 50*(1), 63–99.

Teoh, S. H., Welch, I., & Wong, T. J. (1998b). Earnings management and the long-run market performance of initial public offerings. *Journal of Finance, 53*(6), 1935–1974.

Villalonga, B., & Amit, R. (2010). Family control of firms and industries. *Financial Management, 39*, 863–904.

Walker, M. (2013). How far can we trust earnings numbers? What research tells us about earnings management. *Accounting and Business Research, 43*(4), 445–481.

Wang, D. (2006). Founding family ownership and earnings quality. *Journal of Accounting Research, 44*(3), 619–656.

Watts, R. L., & Zimmerman, J. (1986). *Positive accounting theory*. Englewood Cliffs, NJ: Prentice-Hall.

Yang, M. L. (2010). The impact of controlling families and family CEOs on earnings management. *Family Business Review, 23*(3), 266–279.

Zellweger, T. M., & Dehlen, T. (2012). Value is in the eye of the owner: Affect infusion and socioemotional wealth among family firm owners. *Family Business Review, 25*(3), 280–297.

Chapter 5
Earnings Management, Issues and Firm Market Value

Abstract We address the question of the value relevance of earnings management practices. Using a sample of 239 non-financial listed firms for the period 2007–2015 and drawing on the agency theory integrated with the socioemotional wealth framework we study the effect of earnings quality on a firm's market value. Equity and bond issues are accounted for and we control also for the effect of corporate social responsibility (CSR) disclosure. The results suggest that family and non-family firms' market value is related to different drivers. Earnings management practices have a significant negative effect on non-family firms' market value whilst they do not affect family firms' value in a significant way. We provide also empirical evidence of a significant positive relation between voluntary non-financial disclosure and market value, but this is true only for family firms. The influence exerted by families in terms of founder presence in management, family CEO and family members on the board does not seems to have an impact on firms' market value.

Keywords Earnings management · Accruals · Market value · CSR disclosure · Equity issue · Bond issue · Family firm

5.1 Introduction

Family firms' performance is a very challenging issue. It has engaged research in the area of family business in the past two decades with mixed results. Some studies suggest that family firms outperform non-family businesses (Anderson and Reeb 2003; Barontini and Caprio 2006; Sciascia and Mazzola 2008; San Martin-Reyna and Duran-Encalada 2012), other studies report a negative relation between family control and performance (Cronqvist and Nilsson 2003), while other research does not find significant differences between family and non-family companies' financial performance (Miralles-Marcelo et al. 2014). Literature suggests that this contrasting evidence is affected by a number of interplaying factors among them the different definitions of family business, variables, methodologies and institutional settings

P. Gottardo, A. M. Moisello, *Capital Structure, Earnings Management, and Risk of Financial Distress*, SpringerBriefs in Business,
https://doi.org/10.1007/978-3-030-00344-9_5

used by different authors (Allouche et al. 2008; Maury 2006; Sacristán-Navarro et al. 2011). Different conditions may influence the family effect on performance (Dyer 2018). Family firms are a heterogeneous group, as they differ in terms of governance as well as management, so the socioemotional wealth may be differently related to financial performance. There is evidence that when the firm is led by the founding family and, in particular, in the first generational stage when socioemotional wealth is higher (Gómez-Mejía et al. 2011), family firms perform better than their non-family counterpart (Barontini and Caprio 2006; Villalonga and Amit 2006; Gottardo and Moisello 2015).

There is evidence that financial reporting quality, measured in terms of abnormal discretionary accruals, negatively affects a firm's market performance around equity issues (Rangan 1998; Heron and Lie 2004). Focusing on family firms, we know that they present a higher accounting quality (Cascino et al. 2010) as they are less prone to engage in earnings management (Prencipe et al. 2008; Pazzaglia et al. 2013), but we do not know if their market value is affected by the quality of their disclosure.

This issue is of interest given the ubiquity of family companies in the financial markets across the world and their particular role in Continental Europe Stock Exchanges.

We address this literature gap by analyzing a sample of Italian non-financial listed family and non-family firms during the period 2007–2015, from an Agency Theory perspective integrated with the Socioemotional Wealth framework. We analyze the effect of financial and non-financial disclosure quality on firm value, comparing family and non-family firms. In doing so, we take into account equity and bond issues, a firm's operational, financial and industry-related risk and profitability. We also control for the effect of certain governance and management-related variables such as the presence of the founder in management, of a family CEO, of multiple family members on the board and for a family stake in the business. Overall, on the one hand our results highlight that earnings management strongly affects non-family firms' market value, but the effect is not significant for family firms. On the other hand, our findings suggest that non-financial voluntary disclosure significantly increases market performance only in the case of family firms. Therefore, this research contributes to family business literature by providing evidence on the relevance of family firms' accounting and disclosure choices.

The remainder of the chapter is organized as follows: Sect. 5.2 presents the literary review and hypothesis development; Sects. 5.3 and 5.4 respectively describe methodology and results; Sect. 5.5 discusses the results; Sect. 5.6 concludes by pointing out implications and limitations of this study as well as suggestions for further research.

5.2 Literary Review and Hypothesis Development

5.2.1 Earnings Management and Market Performance

According to the earnings management perspective, managers mislead investors by upward accruals earnings manipulations in order to increase a firm's value when it is raising equity capital. The subsequent reduction of accrual decreases earnings and investors' evaluation of the value of the firm (Heron and Lie 2004). The analysis of accruals manipulations during the year of equity issues shows that this behavior predicts both earnings changes and market-adjusted stock returns in the subsequent year (Rangan 1998). DuCharme et al. (2001) find that pre-IPO abnormal accruals are positively related to a firm's initial value but that their relationship with subsequent company performance is negative. There is evidence that accruals earnings management is unusually high around equity issues, particularly for companies whose issues are going to produce lawsuits (DuCharme et al. 2004). Moreover, the incidence of lawsuits related to stock issues are significantly positively related to abnormal accruals around the offer and significantly negatively related to subsequent stock returns. There is evidence that managers employ both accruals and real earnings management and that they trade off earnings management practices, taking into account their relative costs (Zang 2011). Moreover, since the latter is harder to detect by auditors and government regulators, managers resort to real earnings management as litigation risk increases (Zang 2011).

Effective governance systems enhance a firm's value as they decrease the conflict of interest between minority shareholders and managers of companies and they reduce information asymmetries (Audousset-Coulier et al. 2015). Corporate governance has to guarantee the accountability of top management and, at the same time, ensure management autonomy by providing incentives for acting for the good of the business (Braswell and Daniels 2017). Nazir and Afza 2018 studied the role of corporate governance in increasing a firm's value, taking into account the moderating role of earnings management, and they found that managers' opportunistic attitude to manipulating earnings moderates the positive relationship between governance and firm value.

Graham et al. (2005) provide evidence that CFOs believe that achieving performance benchmarks is key for investors' perceptions of a company value and they also believe that earnings management can increase their evaluations of a firm's value. De Jong et al. (2014) report that analysts share CFOs' opinion on the relevance of achieving benchmarks, but they always deem all earnings manipulation practices to be value-destroying.

H1 Earnings management negatively affects firm value

5.2.2 Family Firm's Performance

Family firms' performance is a challenging issue which has been addressed by a number of scholars without reaching unanimous results. Wagner et al. (2015) performed a meta-analysis, incorporating 380 studies from 41 countries, and pointed out that in 61% of these empirical studies, family governance positively affects a firm's performance, but the picture of family firms' performance is "not entirely unambiguous" (p. 8). This positive effect is stronger when a study is based on a family ownership definition. Nevertheless, Anderson and Reeb (2003) find that the relation between family ownership and performance, measured by Tobin's q as well as by ROA, is not linear: performance increases with the stake of family ownership, but there is an inflection point or maximum performance when family ownership stake reaches 31% of a firm's capital then the relation declines. A meta-analysis conducted by O'Boyle et al. (2012) on 78 papers did not find a significant relation between family involvement and a firm's performance.

Literature on family businesses' performance presents mixed results in terms of family ownership as well as of family management's effect on performance. Some studies on listed firms have found that family firms perform better than non-family firms (Anderson and Reeb 2003; Vieira 2014) while other studies suggest that family control influences profitability, but that family ownership has no significant effect (Sacristán-Navarro et al. 2011). Conversely, Poutziouris et al. (2015) suggest a non-linear relationship between family ownership and performance as they find that performance increases until a family stake reaches 31% but, at this point, performance begins to decline. On the other hand, research suggests that widely-held corporations outperform heirs and founder-led family firms (Morck et al. 1988). According to Miller and Le Breton-Miller (2006) and Chu (2011) family direct involvement in the business has a greater effect on performance than indirect influence by the means of ownership control. Other studies indicate that family firms are better performers only when the founder is alive, and they show that companies led by a descendant family CEO and non-family businesses are not statistically distinguishable (Barontini and Caprio 2006). Research studied the effect of CEO characteristics—belonging to the family or not, founder or descendent—on firm performance and concluded that the owner-manager conflict in non-family firms is costlier than the conflict between family and non-family shareholders in the case of a founder-CEO, but that the effect is reversed when the firm is managed by a descendent-CEO (Villalonga and Amit 2006). Family involvement in the business in terms of management—by means of a family CEO—and of governance—by appointing family members to the board—protect a firm's performance in the long run and across generations (Poutziouris et al. 2015), although there is evidence that descendants may be worse managers than non-family CEOs (Bennedsen and Nielsen 2010). Research also points out that board size and the presence of independent directors on the board affect founder and non-founder managed companies differently (García-Ramos and García-Olalla 2011). Founder-led family firms' performance is negatively related to board size, but it is positively affected by the presence of independent directors. These effects are reversed for non-founder led family businesses. Moreover, there is evidence that CEO duality and board meetings have a significant positive effect when the business is led by descendants (García-Ramos and García-Olalla 2011).

5.2.3 Socioemotional Wealth, Earnings Management and Market Value

A number of studies have analyzed family firms' performance based on the Agency Theory framework (Miller et al. 2007; Sciascia and Mazzola 2008; García-Ramos and García-Olalla 2011; Sacristán-Navarro et al. 2011; Poutziouris et al. 2015). Literature suggests that family firms are affected by agency costs, but that the conflicts generating these negative effects are lower in family than in non-family businesses (Chrisman et al. 2004). As pointed out in the previous chapter, the owner—manager conflict is moderated by the direct involvement of the family on the board or by an indirect influence, by appointing a professional CEO, as well as by the strong monitoring incentives they have as large shareholders (Shleifer and Vishny 1986). Family owners—non-family shareholder conflicts are shaped by families' will to preserve the socioemotional wealth in different and, sometimes, contrasting ways. Gómez-Mejía et al. (2007) studying a sample of Spanish oil mills that were considering whether to join a cooperative, found that families preferred to maintain control over the business rather than to join the cooperative and increase their performance. This suggests that family businesses are prone to jeopardize financial performance and, consequently, non-family shareholders' interest, when family control is at risk. The desire to preserve family control may also result in the appointment of family members to the board, a choice that may infringe rules of good governance (Kellermanns et al. 2012) and affect a firm's market performance. Likewise, family firms are more likely to appoint independent directors linked by friendship with family members or by contractual links with the company (García-Ramos and García-Olalla 2011). This behavior on the one hand may jeopardize board effectiveness and performance (Rubenson and Gupta 1997), on the other hand it reduces the needs for "costly mechanisms for separating the management and control of decisions", it lowers supervision costs and it may increase a firm's value (Fama and Jensen 1983). Family firms are prone to assume performance risk but they avoid venturing risk as it may harm their durability (Gómez-Mejía et al. 2007), and therefore it conflicts with the desire to pass on the business to future generations—a key dimension of the socioemotional wealth (Berrone et al. 2012). There is evidence that a direct influence of the family on the business increases a company's entrepreneurial risk aversion (Huybrechts et al. 2013). The desire "to renew the family bonds to the business by dynastic succession" may have a double-edged effect on performance. On the one hand, it is a strong motivation for preserving and enhancing performance but, on the other, it may put performance at risk when, during succession, a family member "who did not attend selective undergraduate institutions" is appointed CEO (Pérez-González 2006, p. 1559). The SEW dimension related to the sense of identification between the family and the business may affect financial performance in different ways. On the one hand, family members may not pay enough attention to preventing fraud because the family and the company are seen as a unitary entity (Kidwell and Kidwell 2010). Moreover, the strong bonds between family members and the firm might result in organizational norms that deviate from societal standards, fraudulent activities and scandals (Eddleston and Kidwell 2012). On the other hand, families share the sense of identification with the business with non-family employees who become part of a sort of extended family (Berrone et al. 2012). Employees which work for founder-managed family businesses, in which the sense of identification between the family and the business is higher, rate their firms higher than employees of non-family companies, and there is evidence that these assessments are positively related to a firm's subsequent market performance (Huang et al. 2015). Family firms also develop strong ties with a broader set of stakeholders than employees, i.e. suppliers, customers, lenders and the community at large (Berrone et al. 2012). These connections produce emotional wealth for family members and attract endorsement of a company's management, enhancing a firm's as well as an owning family's, reputation (Cennamo et al. 2012; Gavana et al. 2017a). The company is the mirror image of society for the family, therefore families are particularly concerned to preserve the reputation of the firm they own (Dyer and Whetten 2006). These concerns motivate family firms to ensure good performance (Anderson and Reeb 2003).

High-quality financial disclosure has been well assessed by financial markets. The reputational concerns also result in a higher financial reporting quality in family firms as they fear that earnings management may be detected (Prencipe et al. 2008; Cascino et al. 2010; Pazzaglia et al. 2013; Martin et al. 2016; Gavana et al. 2017b). There is evidence that family firms are less affected by earnings management negative effects on reputation as they limit this practice (Martínez-Ferrero et al. 2016). Moreover, founding families have strong monitoring incentives, they tend to limit managers' capability to manipulate earnings, and family firms' long-term perspective moderates the pressure on management for short-term profitability (Jaggi et al. 2009). Other studies provide evidence that family companies are more prone to use high negative discretionary accruals in order to reduce earnings and cut dividends (Achleitner et al. 2014). In so doing they can retain more resources for investments that will increase a company's value.

H2 Family control moderates the relation between earnings management and firm value

5.3 Methodology

5.3.1 *Data*

The analysis in this chapter is based on a dataset of 239 non-financial listed Italian firms covering the period 2007–2015 extracted from AIDA (Italian Digital Database of Companies—*Bureau van Dijk*). Our sample consists of non-financial firms excluding banks and insurance companies given their peculiarities. We collected the data on ownership and governance missing in the AIDA database using public filings from the Italian Stock Exchange and Consob (*Commissione Nazionale per le Società e la Borsa*) websites. Our primary discriminant between family and non-family firms is based on ownership. We define a firm as a family firm if the ultimate owner is a family that owns at least 20% of common shares (Villalonga and Amit 2010). The threshold is consistent with those used in international studies of corporate ownership and facilitates the comparison of our results with those found previously. The threshold used in the literature in the case of listed firms ranges from 5% to 25% (Faccio and Lang 2002; Franks et al. 2011; Ellul 2010; Croci et al. 2011). Nonetheless, our results are largely unaffected by the threshold choice: in fact, observing the data in Table 5.1, it is clearly evident that the family ownership stake is very high in the listed family firms with an average ownership of 60%. In the regression analysis, we control for the degree of family ownership, family involvement in the firm, measured in terms of active family management and presence of multiple family members on the board. This approach allows us to verify if a closer degree of control and influence of the family influence market value.

Table 5.1 Descriptive statistics

	All firms	Family firms	Non-family firms
	Mean (Stdev)	Mean (Stdev)	Mean (Stdev)
Market value	11.55 (1.85)	11.66 (1.82)	11.38 (1.88)
Sus_{t-1}	0.05 (0.18)	0.06 (0.19)	0.05 (0.17)
Age	3.38 (0.67)	3.45 (0.60)	3.29 (0.75)
Beta	0.79 (0.21)	0.79 (0.19)	0.80 (0.23)
Leverage	1.16 (2.09)	1.31 (2.29)	0.97 (1.77)
Roa	2.87 (10.86)	4.26 (8.39)	0.04 (14.24)
Operational leverage	0.77 (2.72)	−0.72 (2.64)	0.84 (2.83)
ABSDA	0.08 (0.10)	0.08 (0.07)	0.10 (0.12)
Equity issues	0.17	0.12	0.24
Bond issues	0.03	0.02	0.03
Family CEO		0.61	
FMulti		2.48 (1.49)	
Founder	0.48	0.56	0.37
QFamily		0.60 (0.15)	

5.3.2 Variables

The dependent variable used in our descriptive statistics and regression models is market value, defined as the log of market capitalization at the end of each year. As for explanatory and control variables, we use the absolute value of discretionary accruals, profitability, leverage, operational leverage, market risk, firm age, CSR disclosure, the presence of the founder, equity and bond issues, a family CEO, multiple family members in the board, the family ownership stake, year dummies.

We assume discretionary accruals as the proxy for earnings management and draw upon the modified Jones model for their estimation and to assess earnings quality (Dechow et al. 1995; Bartov et al. 2000; Peasnell et al. 2000; Subramanyam 1996). The model distinguishes discretionary and non-discretionary accruals, and the absolute discretionary accruals can be used as a proxy for earnings management.

We compute total accruals (TA) using the balance sheet approach as:

$$TA_{i,t} = \Delta CA_{i,t} - \Delta CASH_{i,t} - \Delta CL_{i,t} + \Delta STD_{i,t} - DEP_{i,t} \tag{5.1}$$

with:

$TA_{i,t}$ = total accruals
$\Delta CA_{i,t}$ = change in current assets in year t
$\Delta CASH_{i,t}$ = change in cash and cash equivalents in year t
$\Delta CL_{i,t}$ = change in current liabilities in year t
$\Delta STD_{i,t}$ = change in short-term debts included in current liabilities in year t
$DEP_{i,t}$ = depreciation and amortization expenses

Using the cross-sectional version of the model (Bartov et al. 2000; Peasnell et al. 2000) and grouping our sample firms by industry, retaining only the year-industry with at least ten observations, we estimate the model in Eq. (5.2) for each year-industry from 2007 to 2015, assuming that the financial statement variables represent the drivers of non-discretionary accruals, while the residuals of the model represent the discretionary accruals.

$$\begin{aligned} TA_{i,t}/A_{i,t-1} = {} & \alpha_0 + \alpha_1(1/A_{i,t-1}) + \alpha_2[(\Delta REV_{i,t} - \Delta REC_{i,t})/A_{i,t-1}] \\ & + \alpha_3(PPE_{i,t}/A_{i,t-1}) + \varepsilon_{i,t} \end{aligned} \tag{5.2}$$

where:

$A_{i,t-1}$ = lagged total assets
$\Delta REV_{i,t}$ = change in revenues in year t
$\Delta REC_{i,t}$ = change in trade receivables in year t
$PPE_{i,t}$ = gross property, plant and equipment

The coefficients α_0, α_1, α_2, α_3 in Eq. (5.2) are then applied to estimate non-discretionary accruals for firm i in period t as:

$$NDA_{i,t}/A_{i,t-1} = a_0 + a_1(1/A_{i,t-1}) + a_2[(\Delta REV_{i,t} - \Delta REC_{i,t})/A_{i,t-1}] + a_3(PPE_{i,t}/A_{i,t-1}) \quad (5.3)$$

Since firms can manage earnings either upward or downward we use the absolute value of discretionary accruals (ABSDA) for firm i in period t calculated as the absolute value of the difference between total accruals and non-discretionary accruals to measure earnings quality:

$$ABSDA_{i,t} = | TA_{i,t}/A_{i,t-1} - NDA_{i,t}/A_{i,t-1} | \quad (5.4)$$

Profitability is measured by Roa. Leverage is given by the book value of the financial debt-to-equity ratio. Operational leverage is measured as the ratio of contribution margin to operating income. The proxy for market risk for each year is given by the industry equity beta measured with data in the previous 3 years. Firm age is measured as the log of the number of years since the company was founded. CSR disclosure data was collected from the stand-alone CSR reports available for each firm/year in the sample. The index of disclosure of each firm/year is based on a content analysis, using a grid of items measuring environmental, society, labor practice and product responsibility disclosure consistent with the Global Reporting Initiative (GRI) Sustainability Reporting Guidelines To each firm/year a score of 1 is assigned for a specific item disclosed and 0 otherwise: the total score for a firm/year is the ratio between the sum of the scores and the maximum score relevant for that firm/year, thus excluding the items not relevant for each firm In the regression models the explanatory variable is the disclosure score (SUS) for a firm in year (t-1). Founder is a dummy that takes value 1 if the founder is still present in the firm's management. Equity and bond issues are dummy variables that take value 1 if in a year the firm issued respectively equity or bonds. Family CEO is a dummy assuming value 1 if the CEO is a family member. Fmulty is the number of family members that sit on the board. Family ownership (QFamily) is the sum of the stakes owned by members of the family, we use this variable as a measure of the "family influence and control" dimension of socioemotional wealth (Berrone et al. 2012). Year dummies control for time effects.

5.3.3 Methods

We analyze the impact of earnings management and family control on market value using several statistical approaches. We performed a preliminary correlation analysis to verify the absence of multicollinearity problems for our set of variables. Then we applied a robust panel data analysis. The panel data analysis uses efficiently cross and time-series data increasing the number of observations and the parameter's reliability, reducing also the likelihood of multicollinearity problems. OLS standard errors are unbiased if the residuals are i.i.d. but, if the residuals are correlated across observations, OLS standard errors can be biased. To obtain more efficient estimates we perform a pooling analysis with standard errors adjusted for correlation within a cluster. In our methodology standard errors are clustered by firm. The resulting standard errors are unbiased and produce correct confidence intervals whether the firm effect is temporary or permanent (Petersen 2009). To control for time fixed-effects we include dichotomous variables in the models. The correlations between the independent variables and the variance inflation factors of our regressions are relatively small. We also analyzed the influence diagnostics to detect the presence of outliers. We show the regression models separately for the family and non-family subsamples.

5.4 Results

Table 5.1 presents descriptive statistics of the variables used in this chapter for the full sample and the family and non-family subsamples. Family firms present higher leverage, profitability and lower absolute discretionary accruals, they issue equity and bonds less frequently with respect to non-family firms and their market value and CSR disclosure scores are higher (Figs. 5.1 and 5.2). From the governance point of view, listed family firms show a concentrated ownership. In the Italian family listed firms, the family is well represented in active management through the presence of the founder, multiple family members on the board and a family CEO.

Table 5.2 shows the results of the correlation analysis for the full sample and the main explanatory variables.

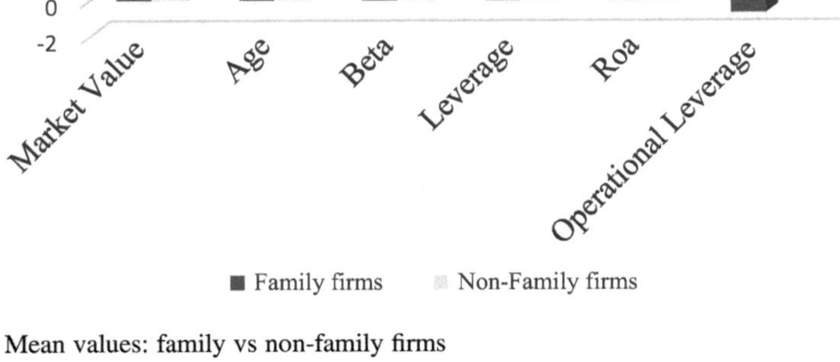

Fig. 5.1 Mean values: family vs non-family firms

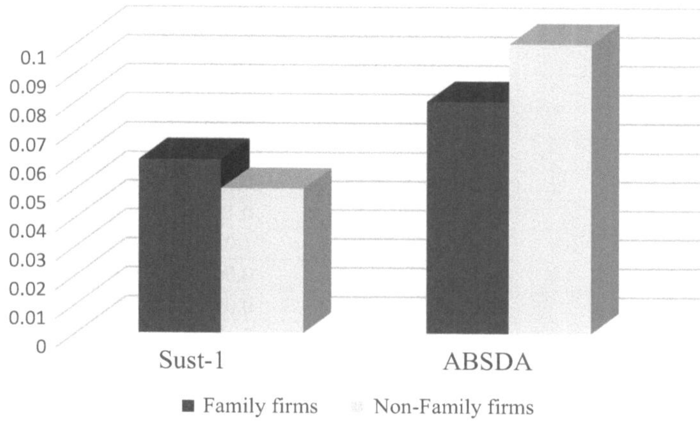

Fig. 5.2 CSR disclosure extent and earnings management (mean values): family vs non-family firms

Table 5.2 Pearson correlation coefficients. Full sample, period 2007–2015

	1	2	3	4	5	6	7	8	9
1. Market value	**1**								
2. Sus_{t-1}	**0.32**								
3. Age	**0.27**	**0.09**							
4. Beta	−0.05	**−0.08**	−0.04						
5. Leverage	**−0.15**	**−0.06**	−0.04	0.01					
6. Roa	**0.17**	**0.06**	−0.05	−0.02	**−0.12**				
7. Operational leverage	0.01	**−0.07**	−0.00	0.02	−0.02	0.05			
8. ABSDA	**−0.15**	−0.00	**−0.07**	−0.02	0.02	**−0.13**	0.01		
9. Equity issues	0.02	−0.03	**−0.10**	0.04	**0.09**	**−0.07**	0.01	**0.08**	
10. Bond issues	**0.09**	**0.09**	0.01	−0.02	0.00	0.01	0.04	0.00	**0.11**

Bold indicates the correlation coefficients significant at the 5% level

Table 5.3 displays the regression results. We performed a panel-data analysis with standard errors clustered at the firm level and with a control for time fixed-effects using dummy variables. The first two columns show a standard model (model 1) for both non-family and family firms, while in the last column we report a second model for the family firms taking into account the governance and the control/influence variables peculiar to the family firms.

The panel results show that the explanatory power of the basic model is quite different for family and non-family firms. The evidence indicates also that family and non-family firms differ markedly in the drivers of their market values. The market value of non-family firms is related to the age of the firm, the emission of equity and bonds and to the earnings management policies, while the drivers of family firm's market value are profitability and past CSR disclosure. Regarding the

Table 5.3 Regression results

	Non-family firms	Family firms	Family firms
	Model 1	Model 1	Model 2
Int	10.52***	10.58***	11.33***
Sus_{t-1}	0.89	3.18***	3.28***
Age	0.60***	0.39	0.30
Beta	−0.62	0.18	0.02
Leverage	−0.02	−0.05	−0.05
Roa	0.01	0.06***	0.06***
Operational leverage	0.00	0.01	0.01
AESDA	−3.71***	0.17	−0.19
Equity issues	0.60*	0.10	0.09
Bond issues	1.64***	0.30	0.49
Family CEO			−0.40
FMulti			0.00
Founder			−0.35
QFamily			0.00
Year dummies	yes	yes	yes
R^2	0.21	0.31	0.34
OBS	288	419	410

***, * indicate significance at the 1% and 10% level respectively

other explanatory variables, leverage, operational leverage and beta are never significant, and it does not seem that the differences within the family firms in terms of governance and family influence have an impact on the results.

5.5 Discussion

Our results suggest that family firms and non-family firms, in terms of market performance, are not statistically distinguishable but that their market value is affected by different variables.

Consistent with these results, we showed in Chap. 2, studying a sample of private and listed firms, that family firms are particularly concerned with the preservation of family control and influence on the business. They are significantly less prone to resort to equity issue than non-family firms. Family firms are also less prone to issue bonds than their non-family counterpart. This is likely to be due to a preference for bank lending as family firms are known to develop strong relations with stakeholders and, among them, lenders; there is evidence that, during the crisis, banks reduced credit less strongly for family than non-family companies (D'Aurizio et al. 2015). Moreover, our results suggest that family firms rely on higher internally-produced financial resources as indicated by ROA. Investments and growth financing depend more on equity and bond issues in non-family than family companies, and this explain why we find emissions to have a significant effect only for non-family firms' market value. Consistent with this view, our results show that family companies' market value is strongly affected by a firm's operative performance. Further, our results show that family firms market value is not affected by the type of influence the family exerts on the business as the presence of the founder, of a family CEO or of multiple family members on the board, do not affect a firm's market value. Our findings suggest that family ownership control on the business determines the effect, of the variables taken in consideration, on firm value, although the measure of a family stake in a firm does not significantly affect market value. This result is likely to be due to the high family ownership concentration in Italian listed firms: as we reported in the previous chapter they present a mean value of 59.6% with a low standard deviation and there is evidence that in Italy, as well as in France and Germany, family ownership has a strong inertia towards change (Franks et al. 2011).

The quality of disclosure affects market values of family and non-family firms very differently. Consistent with previous research conducted on earnings management around equity issues, we find that earnings manipulation, by means of abnormal discretionary accruals, has a strong negative effect on non-family firms' market value regardless of previous issuing activity. This result confirms H1, which posited a negative effect of earnings manipulation on firm value. Moreover, our findings show that this effect does not hold in the case of family firms, confirming H2, which supposed family control as moderating the relation between earnings management and a firm's financial performance.

Our findings show that family firms are less prone to engage in earnings manipulation because they are aware of the negative consequences that they would experience if it was detected. It would jeopardize stakeholders' trust and, consequently, family firms' network of relations from which the owning family derives non-financial returns as well as economic and financial advantages for the business. The results of the study we presented in the previous chapter indicate that family firms present lower abnormal discretionary accruals than non-family firms, even in equity issues, because of the reputational concerns related to an enhanced probability of incurring shareholder lawsuits (DuCharme et al. 2004). According to Pazzaglia et al. (2013) the will to preserve socioemotional wealth enhances a firm's quality of mandatory financial information. Family firms are particularly concerned with their image, they pursue a good reputation and, in doing so, they reach a better reputation than non-family firms, as found by Deephouse and Jaskiewicz (2013) in their study on a sample of large companies operating in different countries and cultures. So, family firms present a higher quality of financial disclosure and enjoy a better reputation and, consequently, earnings management does not significantly affect their market value. Conversely, our results suggest that family firms' value is significantly increased by CSR reporting extent, whilst this type of voluntary non-financial disclosure does not significantly enhance non-family companies' market value. These results are consistent with very recent research on CSR, reporting marketing effectiveness in family and non-family companies (Gavana et al. 2018), which points out that this type of communication has a positive significant effect on revenues only for family firms. According to Yoon et al.

(2006), individuals are less prone to trust in self-interested than in neutral communication and they are skeptical about CSR information directly provided by a company (Szykman et al. 2004). Literature suggests that stakeholders evaluate a company's CSR commitment by taking into account its reputation (Du et al. 2010), so we may suppose that investors also assess a firm's CSR disclosure through the lens of its reputation and, for this reason, CSR reporting significantly enhances family firms market' value.

5.6 Implications, Limitations and Avenues for Future Research

This study analyzes the relation between issues, as well as earnings management, and firm value comparing family and non-family firms. Our results indicate that, given family firms' higher economic performance and availability of bank lending, equity and bond issues do not significantly affect a family business' market value. Family firms present a better earnings quality than non-family companies and their market value is not significantly affected by earnings manipulations. Our results indicate that non-family firms present a lower earnings quality and that their market value is negatively affected by this unethical practice. These findings have important implications as they indicate that investors do detect the lower quality of disclosure, regardless of whether issues are present. Conversely, non-financial voluntary disclosure quality has a significant positive relation with family firms' value. These results have relevant implications for family firms as they indicate that CSR reporting is an effective communication tool with investors as they positively evaluate environmental and social voluntary disclosure. A main limitation of this study is that we do not take into consideration the human motivations and social and political conditions which may moderate the above effect. The personal, cultural and social characteristics of their governance are a relevant source of heterogeneity in family firms, therefore further research could deepen the effect of these characteristics on a firm's disclosure quality and its assessment by investors in order to identify under what conditions disclosure quality enhances a firm's market value.

References

Achleitner, A. K., Günther, N., Kaserer, C., & Siciliano, G. (2014). Real earnings management and accrual-based earnings management in family firms. *European Accounting Review, 23*(3), 431–461.

Allouche, J., Amann, B., Jaussaud, J., & Kurashina, T. (2008). The impact of family control on the performance and financial characteristics of family versus nonfamily businesses in Japan: a matched-pair investigation. *Family Business Review, 21*(4), 315–329.

Anderson, R. C., & Reeb, D. M. (2003). Founding-family ownership and firm performance: evidence from the S&P 500. *Journal of Finance, 58*(3), 1301–1328.

Audousset-Coulier, S., Jeny, A., & Jiang, L. (2015). The validity of auditor industry specialization measures. *Auditing: A Journal of Practice & Theory, 35*(1), 139–161.

Barontini, R., & Caprio, L. (2006). The effect of family control on firm value and performance: Evidence from continental Europe. *European Financial Management, 12*(5), 689–723.

Bartov, E., Gul, F. A., & Tsui, J. S. (2000). Discretionary-accruals models and audit qualifications. *Journal of Accounting and Economics, 30*(3), 421–452.

Bennedsen, M., & Nielsen, K. (2010). Incentive and entrenchment effects in European ownership. *Journal of Banking & Finance, 34*, 2212–2229.

Berrone, P., Cruz, C., & Gómez-Mejía, L. R. (2012). Socioemotional wealth in family firms: Theoretical dimensions, assessment approaches, and agenda for future research. *Family Business Review, 25*(3), 258–279.

Braswell, M., & Daniels, R. B. (2017). Alternative Earnings Management Techniques: What Audit Committees and Internal Auditors Should Know. *Journal of Corporate Accounting & Finance, 28*(2), 45–54.

Cascino, S., Pugliese, A., Mussolino, D., & Sansone, C. (2010). The influence of family ownership on the quality of accounting information. *Family Business Review, 23*(3), 246–265.

Cennamo, C., Berrone, P., Cruz, C., & Gómez-Mejía, L. R. (2012). Socioemotional wealth and proactive stakeholder engagement: why family-controlled firms care more about their stakeholders. *Entrepreneurship Theory and Practice, 36*(6), 1153–1173.

Chrisman, J. J., Chua, J. H., & Litz, R. A. (2004). Comparing the agency costs of family and non-family firms: Conceptual issues and exploratory evidence. *Entrepreneurship Theory and Practice, 28*(4), 335–354.

Chu, W. (2011). Family ownership and firm performance: Influence of family management, family control, and firm size. *Asia Pacific Journal of Management, 28*(4), 833–851.

Croci, E., Doukas, J. A., & Gonenc, H. (2011). Family control and financing decisions. *European Financial Management, 17*(5), 860–897.

Cronqvist, H., & Nilsson, M. (2003). Agency costs of controlling minority shareholders. *Journal of Financial and Quantitative Analysis, 38*(4), 695–719.

D'Aurizio, L., Oliviero, T., & Romano, L. (2015). Family firms, soft information and bank lending in a financial crisis. *Journal of Corporate Finance, 33*, 279–292.

De Jong, A., Mertens, G., van der Poel, M., & van Dijk, R. (2014). How does earnings management influence investor's perceptions of firm value? Survey evidence from financial analysts. *Review of Accounting Studies, 19*(2), 606–627.

Dechow, P. M., Sloan, R. G., & Sweeney, A. P. (1995). Detecting earnings management. *Accounting Review, 70*, 193–225.

Deephouse, D. L., & Jaskiewicz, P. (2013). Do family firms have better reputations than non-family firms? An integration of socioemotional wealth and social identity theories. *Journal of Management Studies, 50*(3), 337–360.

Du, S., Bhattacharya, C. B., & Sen, S. (2010). Maximizing business returns to corporate social responsibility (CSR): The role of CSR communication. *International Journal of Management Reviews, 12*(1), 8–19.

DuCharme, L. L., Malatesta, P. H., & Sefcik, S. E. (2001). Earnings management: IPO valuation and subsequent performance. *Journal of Accounting, Auditing & Finance, 16*(4), 369–396.

DuCharme, L. L., Malatesta, P. H., & Sefcik, S. E. (2004). Earnings management, stock issues, and shareholder lawsuits. *Journal of Financial Economics, 71*(1), 27–49.

Dyer, W. G. (2018). Are Family Firms Really Better? Reexamining "Examining the 'Family Effect'on Firm Performance". *Family Business Review, 31*(2), 240–248.

Dyer, W. G., & Whetten, D. A. (2006). Family firms and social responsibility: Preliminary evidence from the S&P 500. *Entrepreneurship Theory and Practice, 30*(6), 785–802.

Eddleston, K. A., & Kidwell, R. E. (2012). Parent–child relationships: Planting the seeds of deviant behavior in the family firm. *Entrepreneurship Theory and Practice, 36*(2), 369–386.

Ellul, A. (2010). *Control motivations and capital structure decision, Working Paper*. Bloomington, IN: Indiana University, Kelley School of Business.

Faccio, M., & Lang, L. H. (2002). The ultimate ownership of Western European corporations. *Journal of Financial Economics, 65*(3), 365–395.

Fama, E. F., & Jensen, M. C. (1983). Agency problems and residual claims. *Journal of Law and Economics, 26*(2), 327–349.

Franks, J., Mayer, C., Volpin, P., & Wagner, H. F. (2011). The life cycle of family ownership: International evidence. *Review of Financial Studies, 25*(6), 1675–1712.

García-Ramos, R., & García-Olalla, M. (2011). Board characteristics and firm performance in public founder-and nonfounder-led family businesses. *Journal of Family Business Strategy, 2*(4), 220–231.

Gavana, G., Gottardo, P., & Moisello, A. M. (2017a). Sustainability reporting in family firms: A panel data analysis. *Sustainability, 9*(1), 38.

Gavana, G., Gottardo, P., & Moisello, A. M. (2017b). Earnings Management and CSR Disclosure. Family vs. Non-Family Firms. *Sustainability, 9*(12), 2327.

Gavana, G., Gottardo, P., & Moisello, A. M. (2018). Do Customers Value CSR Disclosure? Evidence from Italian Family and Non-Family Firms. *Sustainability, 10*(5), 1642.

Gómez-Mejía, L. R., Haynes, K. T., Nunez-Nickel, M., Jacobson, K. J. L., & Moyano-Fuentes, J. (2007). Socioemotional wealth and business risks in family-controlled firms, evidence from Spanish olive oil mills. *Administrative Science Quarterly, 52*(1), 106–137.

Gómez-Mejía, L. R., Cruz, C., Berrone, P., & De Castro, J. (2011). The bind that ties: Socioemotional wealth preservation in family firms. *Academy of Management Annals, 5*(1), 653–707.

Gottardo, P., & Moisello, A. M. (2015). The impact of socioemotional wealth on family firms' financial performance. *Problems and Perspectives in Management, 13*(1), 67–77.

Graham, J. R., Harvey, C. R., & Rajgopal, S. (2005). The economic implications of corporate financial reporting. *Journal of Accounting and Economics, 40*(1–3), 3–73.

Heron, R. A., & Lie, E. (2004). A comparison of the motivations for and the information content of different types of equity offerings. *Journal of Business, 77*(3), 605–632.

Huang, M., Li, P., Meschke, F., & Guthrie, J. P. (2015). Family firms, employee satisfaction, and corporate performance. *Journal of Corporate Finance, 34*, 108–127.

Huybrechts, J., Voordeckers, W., & Lybaert, N. (2013). Entrepreneurial risk taking of private family firms: The influence of a nonfamily CEO and the moderating effect of CEO tenure. *Family Business Review, 26*(2), 161–179.

Jaggi, B., Leung, S., & Gul, F. (2009). Family control, board independence and earnings management: Evidence based on Hong Kong firms. *Journal of Accounting and Public Policy, 28*(4), 281–300.

Kellermanns, F. W., Eddleston, K. A., & Zellweger, T. M. (2012). Article Commentary: Extending the Socioemotional Wealth Perspective: A Look at the Dark Side. *Entrepreneurship Theory and Practice, 36*(6), 1175–1182.

Kidwell, L. A., & Kidwell, R. E. (2010). Fraud in the family: How family firm characteristics can shape illegal behavior. In: *Conference paper, August 2010. Conference: American Accounting Association Annual Meeting*.

Martin, G., Campbell, J. T., & Gómez-Mejía, L. R. (2016). Family control, socioemotional wealth and earnings management in publicly traded firms. *Journal of Business Ethics, 133*(3), 453–469.

Martínez-Ferrero, J., Rodríguez-Ariza, L., & Bermejo-Sánchez, M. (2016). Consequences of earnings management for corporate reputation. Evidence from family firms. *Accounting Research Journal, 29*(4), 457–474.

Maury, B. (2006). Family ownership and firm performance: Empirical evidence from Western European corporations. *Journal of Corporate Finance, 12*(2), 321–341.

Miller, D., & Le Breton-Miller, I. (2006). Family governance and firm performance: Agency, stewardship, and capabilities. *Family Business Review, 19*(1), 73–87.

Miller, D., Le Breton-Miller, I., Lester, R. H., & Cannella Jr., A. A. (2007). Are family firms really superior performers? *Journal of Corporate Finance, 13*(5), 829–858.

Miralles-Marcelo, J. L., del Mar Miralles-Quirós, M., & Lisboa, I. (2014). The impact of family control on firm performance: Evidence from Portugal and Spain. *Journal of Family Business Strategy, 5*(2), 156–168.

Morck, R., Shleifer, A., & Vishny, R. (1988). Management ownership and market valuation, an empirical analysis. *Journal of Financial Economics, 20*, 293–315.

Nazir, M. S., & Afza, T. (2018). Does managerial behavior of managing earnings mitigate the relationship between corporate governance and firm value? Evidence from an emerging market. *Future Business Journal, 4*(1), 139–156.

O'Boyle Jr., E. H., Pollack, J. M., & Rutherford, M. W. (2012). Exploring the relation between family involvement and firms' financial performance: A meta-analysis of main and moderator effects. *Journal of Business Venturing, 27*(1), 1–18.

Pazzaglia, F., Mengoli, S., & Sapienza, E. (2013). Earnings quality in acquired and non-acquired family firms: A socioemotional wealth perspective. *Family Business Review, 26*(4), 374–386.

Peasnell, K. V., Pope, P. F., & Young, S. (2000). Detecting earnings management using cross-sectional abnormal accruals models. *Accounting and Business Research, 30*(4), 313–326.

Pérez-González, F. (2006). Inherited control and firm performance. *American Economic Review, 96*(5), 1559–1588.

Petersen, M. A. (2009). Estimating standard errors in finance panel data sets: Comparing approaches. *Review of Financial Studies, 22*(1), 435–480.

Poutziouris, P., Savva, C. S., & Hadjielias, E. (2015). Family involvement and firm performance: Evidence from UK listed firms. *Journal of Family Business Strategy, 6*(1), 14–32.

Prencipe, A., Markarian, G., & Pozza, L. (2008). Earnings management in family firms: Evidence from R&D cost capitalization in Italy. *Family Business Review, 21*(1), 71–88.

Rangan, S. (1998). Earnings management and the performance of seasoned equity offerings. *Journal of Financial Economics, 50*(1), 101–122.

Rubenson, G. C., & Gupta, A. K. (1997). The initial succession: A contingency model of founder tenure. *Entrepreneurship Theory and Practice, 21*(2), 21–36.

Sacristán-Navarro, M., Gómez-Ansón, S., & Cabeza-García, L. (2011). Family ownership and control, the presence of other large shareholders, and firm performance: Further evidence. *Family Business Review, 24*(1), 71–93.

San Martin-Reyna, J. M., & Duran-Encalada, J. A. (2012). The relationship among family business, corporate governance and firm performance: Evidence from the Mexican stock exchange. *Journal of Family Business Strategy, 3*(2), 106–117.

Sciascia, S., & Mazzola, P. (2008). Family involvement in ownership and management: Exploring nonlinear effects on performance. *Family Business Review, 21*(4), 331–345.

Shleifer, A., & Vishny, R. W. (1986). Large shareholders and corporate control. *Journal of Political Economy, 94*(3, Part 1), 461–488.

Subramanyam, K. R. (1996). The pricing of discretionary accruals. *Journal of Accounting and Economics, 22*, 249–281.

Szykman, L. R., Bloom, P. N., & Blazing, J. (2004). Does corporate sponsorship of a socially-oriented message make a difference? An investigation of the effects of sponsorship identity on responses to an anti-drinking and driving message. *Journal of Consumer Psychology, 14*(1–2), 13–20.

Vieira, E. F. S. (2014). The effect on the performance of listed family and non-family firms. *Managerial Finance, 40*(3), 234–253.

Villalonga, B., & Amit, R. (2006). How do family ownership, control and management affect firm value? *Journal of Financial Economics, 80*(2), 385–417.

Villalonga, B., & Amit, R. (2010). Family control of firms and industries. *Financial Management, 39*(3), 863–904.

Wagner, D., Block, J. H., Miller, D., Schwens, C., & Xi, G. (2015). A meta-analysis of the financial performance of family firms: Another attempt. *Journal of Family Business Strategy, 6*(1), 3–13.

Yoon, Y., Gürhan-Canli, Z., & Schwarz, N. (2006). The effect of corporate social responsibility (CSR) activities on companies with bad reputations. *Journal of Consumer Psychology, 16*(4), 377–390.

Zang, A. Y. (2011). Evidence on the trade-off between real activities manipulation and accrual-based earnings management. *Accounting Review, 87*(2), 675–703.

Chapter 6
Conclusions

Abstract This book focuses the effect of family control and influence on some aspects of family firms' financial behavior. The first chapter introduces the theoretical framework, literature overview and the research questions. The second chapter analyzes the effect of family members' affective endowments on a firm's leverage. The third chapter studies the effect of leverage on a company's likelihood of financial distress, pointing out the moderating effect of the owning family's involvement in the business. The fourth chapter addresses the issue of family firms' earnings management practices around equity and bond issues whilst the fifth chapter analyzes the effect of disclosure quality on a firm's market value, taking into account equity and bond issues. This chapter concludes the book, providing an overview of the research, pointing out the main implications and contribution. It also discusses the limitation of our work and provides suggestions for further advances.

6.1 Introduction

Our research develops the issue of family firms' financial behavior. This field of study is attracting the attention of a growing number of scholars because of the fundamental role family firms play across financial markets and economies all over the world. It analyzes the relations between capital structure choices, probability of financial distress and earnings management practices and performance, with the aim of elucidating the differences between family and non-family firms and the effects of different forms of family influence. We develop our research drawing on the Socioemotional wealth integrated with traditional financial theories, because, as suggested by quite recent literature (Gómez-Mejía et al. 2007; Berrone et al. 2012), the pursuit of non-financial goals characterizes family firms' behavior. After a broad review of the available theoretical and empirical literature, we proceed to focus distinctly on the above topics. We review prior research, identify gaps in literature, and test our hypotheses by analyzing longitudinal data on Italian family and non-family non-financial firms. We chose to begin our research by addressing the

P. Gottardo, A. M. Moisello, *Capital Structure, Earnings Management, and Risk of Financial Distress*, SpringerBriefs in Business,
https://doi.org/10.1007/978-3-030-00344-9_6

question of family control and influence effect on capital structure choices. As recently pointed out by Michiels and Molly (2017), financing choices are a relevant and timely issue for family firms, as demonstrated by EU policies that consider access to financial resources a key aspect for family companies' durability and growth. Therefore, we proceed by analyzing the moderating effect of different forms of family involvement in the business on the relation between a firm's leverage and the probability of encountering financial distress. Given the relevance of financial reporting as a source of information for external capital providers, we develop our research by analyzing family firms' accounting choices, in terms of earnings quality, around equity and bond issues, taking into account different forms of family influence on the business. We complete our study by focusing on the effect of disclosure quality on a firm's financial performance, measured in terms of market value. We discuss in detail the findings, implications and avenues for future studies in each chapter. In the conclusion of this work, we take the opportunity to provide a broader interpretation of our findings and widen the suggestions for future research advanced in previous chapters. The reminder of the chapter is organized as follows: Sect. 6.2 provides an overview of the study carried out, pointing out implications and its contribution. In so doing, it highlights the implications of family members' affective endowment in the business, analyzed from the perspective of different financial theories; Sect. 6.3 discusses the limitation of this work and suggests lines of development for further research.

6.2 Research Overview

We draw our analyses on the Socioemotional wealth approach, integrating it with financial theories such as Pecking Order Theory (POT), Trade-off Theory (TOT), and Agency Theory. Although these traditional finance theories have been used as a reference point by relevant literature on family businesses' financing decisions, some concerns have been pointed out in relation to their capability, as stand-alone theories, to explain family firms' behavior, the differences to non-family companies and among family firms (Michiels and Molly 2017; Migliori et al. 2018). The above-mentioned theories assume that capital structure choices are led by the will to maximize companies' financial wealth. Agency Theory explains financial choices as the result of information asymmetries and agency costs between shareholders and management and among different types of shareholder (Jensen and Meckling 1976). According to Trade-off Theory, a firm's leverage ratio is the result of a costs and benefits analysis of debt, which are, in part, related to information asymmetries between shareholders and lenders (Myers 1989). Pecking Order Theory (Myers 1984; Myers and Majluf 1984) posits a preference order in using self-financing, debt and external equity capital, based on information asymmetries costs between a company and capital suppliers. Family firms' behavior is distinctly affected by non-financial goals that may significantly modify information asymmetries and agency costs and, other things being equal, leverage. Socioemotional wealth is a powerful theoretical framework which effectively integrates traditional capital structure theories interpreting the financing decisions of family firms. It explains the differences in leverage between family and non-family businesses and family firms' heterogeneity. The findings illustrated and discussed in Chap. 2 suggest that SEW's salience varies depending on certain characteristics of the firm, i.e. multiple family members on the board, generational stage and ownership dispersion, which affect emotional and social benefits and lead to different financial behaviors. The findings also indicate that, overall, family firms are more levered than non-family companies. The pioneer study of Gómez-Mejía et al. (2007) concludes that family firms are risk adverse and risk-taking at the same time: they are prone to assume the risk of a lower financial result in order to preserve family control as they believe that they can manage performance risk. Consistently, we find that family firms are willing to bear the financial risk related to higher leverage because they are also well equipped to handle this risk. Literature suggests that, due to the strength of their relations with financial institutions, their alignment with lenders towards debt compliance goals and their reputation, they may rely on better and easier financing conditions (Anderson et al. 2003; Chua et al. 2011; Yen et al. 2015; Ma et al. 2017; Hillier et al. 2018).

Under a TOT perspective, socioemotional wealth may alter the balance between debt costs and benefits, according to the salience of its dimensions. Costs refer to the financial and emotional risks related to debt and a consequent increased likelihood of financial distress and bankruptcy, but this risk is moderated by the effect that family involvement in the business exerts on the relation with lenders. Family businesses do not evaluate only the financial benefits of the debt related to taxation, but they attach great value to the protection of control.

From a POT point of view, the preservation of socioemotional wealth aligns family firms' behavior with debt-holder goals: in doing so, it reduces the information asymmetries between family companies and lenders, increasing a firm's preference for debt.

This research provides evidence that family firms present better-quality information for investors as they are less prone to engage in earnings management (Chap. 4). The sense of identification between the family and the business develops a robust concern for reputation in family firms and it positively affects family firms' disclosure quality. Moreover, the presence of the founder and visibility both increase a firm's earnings quality as the former enhances the sense of identification between the family and the business and the latter amplifies the reputational drawbacks related to earnings manipulations (Gavana et al. 2017). Nevertheless, diverse forms of visibility may have a different effect on financial disclosure quality. Financial press exposure increases earnings manipulation and is likely to be due to greater pressure on financial performance endured by more visible companies. Our results suggest that family firms do not manipulate earnings in order to facilitate bond issues and, in instances of equity offerings, they are less prone to engage in earnings management than non-family companies. These results have relevant implications for investors because of earnings manipulations' potentially damaging effect on their investments' performance. Consistently, in Chap. 5, taking into account the effect of debt and equity issues, we provide evidence that family-firms' market value is not affected by earnings management practices whilst discretionary abnormal accruals significantly lower non-family firms' market performance. This has an important implication as it suggests that investors are able to perceive the possible poor quality of the disclosure and this has an effect on the market value of the companies.

Consequently, the system of a family firm's non-financial goals shapes its leverage: control motivations determine debt preference, reputation and the development of social relations' objectives facilitate the raising of debt capital. As a result, some SEW moderators, such as the degree of family involvement in the business, generational stage and ownership dispersion, affect leverage (Chap. 2).

Our research highlights that direct family involvement in a firm's management facilitates debt management and the financial risk related to leverage (Chap. 3). The findings we present in Chap. 3 show that leverage increases family and non-family businesses' likelihood of financial distress, but that the presence of a family CEO significantly moderates this effect. Literature report that family firms, given their will to pass on the business to future generations and the related long-term perspective (Berrone et al. 2012), prefer long-term loans (Steijvers and Voordeckers 2016) as they imply a lower financial risk (Ortiz-Molina and Penas 2008; Mishra and McConaughy 1999). A family's direct involvement enhances the pursuit of the SEW dimensions (Gómez-Mejía et al. 2011)—family control and influence preservation, sense of identification between the family and the business and the desire to renew the bond between the former and the latter though dynastic succession—and it reinforces the motivations underlying the choice of less risky forms of debt financing. On the other hand, the presence of the family in management facilitates relations with financial institutions, ensuring bank lending even during periods of crisis (D'Aurizio et al. 2015).

The salience of SEW in capital structure choices has relevant implications for regulators. The Italian equity market is very limited in terms of the number of publicly-listed firms as well as of capitalization, even compared to France and Germany, which are insider systems just like Italy. Franks et al. (2011) report that Italian family businesses have a particular inertia in diluting a company's control, again in comparison to firms operating in the above-mentioned countries. So, these findings, taken together, suggest that family companies' aversion to open up capital to outsiders plays a relevant role in the poor development of the Italian financial market. Therefore, effective measures are needed by regulatory bodies in order to reduce concerns about external investors and stimulate the development of the equity market.

Our research contributes to family firm literature by suggesting that the Socioemotional wealth approach, integrated with traditional financial theories, provides an effective framework in explaining family businesses' financial choices, disclosure and performance.

6.3 Future Research

This research concentrates on an Italian setting, one that is a very interesting context for studying the financial behaviour of family firms given family firms' relevance in Italy, a country characterized by a bank-based economy. The choice between debt and equity is also affected by the characteristics of the financial system in terms of the relative importance of banks versus capital markets. Therefore, it is necessary to extend the analysis to an international dataset, integrating the model to account for the different national environments in terms of cultural elements, which may have a moderating effect on pursuing socioemotional wealth, controlling for institutional context and capital market development. Italy is an insider or bank-oriented system with different characteristics compared to outsider or market-oriented systems, like the USA and UK. The presence of independent directors, the strict separation of chairman and CEO, the balance of power between shareholders and management, deviations from the one-share-one-vote principle, investor and minority shareholder protection, the development of financial markets and the presence of an active market for corporate control, vary greatly across countries and they must be explicitly taken into account in a cross-country analysis. Moreover, the different dimensions that characterize a national cultural context shape the interactions between individuals, and the behavior and the choices of the organization in which they operate (Basco et al. 2018). The role of the family differs across cultural contexts and it may affect the salience of socioemotional wealth and the control motivation in leverage choices in addition to a family firm's capability to rely on the personal relationship between family members and financial institutions and to manage leverage-related risks.

Our results suggest that having multiple family members on the board increases leverage, but it does not moderate the effect of the latter on the probability of financial distress. Our findings show that a family CEO lowers this effect. More detailed studies are needed in order to understand under what conditions family involvement enhances leverage, or it reduces the effect of leverage on the likelihood of encountering financial distress. Family firms are a heterogeneous group (Chua et al. 2012), they may differ in terms of type of involvement in the firm and generational stage as well as owning family structure (traditional nuclear family or other non-traditional structure), events which characterize family life or interactions between family members (Dyer 2018; Dyer et al. 2014). These factors may play a mediating or moderating role in capital structure choices or in the relation between leverage and the probability of financial distress, as well as on financial disclosure quality and its effect on a firm's market value. The very recent study by Calabrò et al. (2018), on family firms' succession choices, points out that the effect of a family's interactions and norms in choosing future leaders affects a firm's performance. Therefore, taking into account these aspects would be a promising avenue for developing the study of the relations we discuss in this book.

Our study focuses on the effect of "family control and influence" dimension of the SEW on certain financial and disclosure choices. We measure SEW indirectly, relying on proxies suggested by literature (Berrone et al. 2012): family ownership and involvement in management, which are potential drivers of a family member's affective endowment in the business (Schulze and Kellermanns 2015). These proxies are unable to capture the multidimensionality of SEW, which also consists of other relevant dimensions: "identification of family members with the firm", "binding social ties", "emotional attachment of family members" and "renewal of family bond to the firm through dynastic succession" (Berrone et al. 2012). These dimensions play a relevant role in shaping a firm's risk-taking behavior, its concern for reputation, its attitude to be compliant with debt contracts—and, more in general, with norms—and its capability to develop relations with financial institutions. Scholars suggest a more detailed measure of SEW (Debicki et al. 2016), in order to effectively take into account the multidimensionality of the affective endowment and its heterogeneity among family firms (Miller and Le Breton-Miller 2014; Chua et al. 2015). Hence, it could be of interest to address the research questions suggested by this book using a more specific measure of SEW, as advanced by literature (Hauck et al. 2016), to directly measure the variations of the affective endowment in the firm and better analyze their effect on a firm's financial and disclosure behavior.

References

Anderson, R. C., Mansi, S. A., & Reeb, D. M. (2003). Founding family ownership and the agency cost of debt. *Journal of Financial Economics, 68*(2), 263–285.

Basco, R., Calabrò, A., & Campopiano, G. (2018). Transgenerational entrepreneurship around the world: Implications for family business research and practice. *Journal of Family Business Strategy*. https://doi.org/10.1016/j.jfbs.2018.03.004.

Berrone, P., Cruz, C., & Gómez-Mejía, L. R. (2012). Socioemotional wealth in family firms: Theoretical dimensions, assessment approaches, and agenda for future research. *Family Business Review, 25*(3), 258–279.

Calabrò, A., Minichilli, A., Amore, M. D., & Brogi, M. (2018). The courage to choose! Primogeniture and leadership succession in family firms. *Strategic Management Journal, 39*, 2014–2035.

Chua, J. H., Chrisman, J. J., Kellermanns, F. W., & Wu, Z. (2011). Family involvement and new venture debt financing. *Journal of Business Venturing, 26*(4), 472–488.

Chua, J. H., Chrisman, J. J., Steier, L. P., & Rau, S. B. (2012). Sources of heterogeneity in family firms: An introduction. *Entrepreneurship Theory and Practice, 36*(6), 1103–1113.

Chua, J. H., Chrisman, J. J., & De Massis, A. (2015). A closer look at socioemotional wealth: Its flows, stocks, and prospects for moving forward. *Entrepreneurship Theory and Practice, 39*(2), 173–182.

D'Aurizio, L., Oliviero, T., & Romano, L. (2015). Family firms, soft information and bank lending in a financial crisis. *Journal of Corporate Finance, 33*, 279–292.

Debicki, B. J., Kellermanns, F. W., Chrisman, J. J., Pearson, A. W., & Spencer, B. A. (2016). Development of a socioemotional wealth importance (SEWi) scale for family firm research. *Journal of Family Business Strategy, 7*(1), 47–57.

Dyer, W. G. (2018). Are family firms really better? Reexamining "examining the 'family effect'on firm performance". *Family Business Review, 31*(2), 240–248.

Dyer, W. G., Nenque, E., & Hill, E. J. (2014). Toward a theory of family capital and entrepreneurship: Antecedents and outcomes. *Journal of Small Business Management, 52*(2), 266–285.

Franks, J., Mayer, C., Volpin, P., & Wagner, H. F. (2011). The life cycle of family ownership: International evidence. *Review of Financial Studies, 25*(6), 1675–1712.

Gavana, G., Gottardo, P., & Moisello, A. M. (2017). Earnings management and CSR disclosure. Family vs. non-family firms. *Sustainability, 9*(12), 2327.

Gómez-Mejía, L. R., Haynes, K. T., Nunez-Nickel, M., Jacobson, K. J. L., & Moyano-Fuentes, J. (2007). Socioemotional wealth and business risks in family-controlled firms: Evidence from Spanish olive oil mills. *Administrative Science Quarterly, 52*, 106–137.

Gómez-Mejía, L. R., Cruz, C., Berrone, P., & De Castro, J. (2011). The bind that ties: Socioemotional wealth preservation in family firms. *Academy of Management Annals, 5*(1), 653–707.
Hauck, J., Suess-Reyes, J., Beck, S., Prügl, R., & Frank, H. (2016). Measuring socioemotional wealth in family-owned and-managed firms: A validation and short form of the FIBER scale. *Journal of Family Business Strategy, 7*(3), 133–148.
Hillier, D., Martínez, B., Patel, P. C., Pindado, J., & Requejo, I. (2018). Pound of flesh? Debt contract strictness and family firms. *Entrepreneurship Theory and Practice, 42*(2), 259–282.
Jensen, M. C., & Meckling, W. H. (1976). Theory of the firm: Managerial behavior, agency costs and ownership structure. *Journal of Financial Economics, 3*(4), 305–360.
Ma, L., Ma, S., & Tian, G. (2017). Corporate opacity and cost of debt for family firms. *European Accounting Review, 26*, 27–59.
Michiels, A., & Molly, V. (2017). Financing decisions in family businesses: A review and suggestions for developing the field. *Family Business Review, 30*(4), 369–399.
Migliori, S., Maturo, F., & Paolone, F. (2018). Capital structure determinants in family firms: An empirical analysis in context of crisis. *International Business Research, 11*(4), 65.
Miller, D., & Le Breton-Miller, I. (2014). Deconstructing socioemotional wealth. *Entrepreneurship Theory and Practice, 38*(4), 713–720.
Mishra, C. S., & McConaughy, D. L. (1999). Founding family control and capital structure: The risk of loss of control and the aversion to debt. *Entrepreneurship Theory and Practice, 23*(4), 53–53.
Myers, S. C. (1984). The capital structure puzzle. *Journal of Finance, 39*(3), 574–592.
Myers, S. C. (1989). Still searching for optimal capital structure. Are the distinctions between debt and equity disappearing. *Journal of Applied Corporate Finance, 13*, 80–95.
Myers, S. C., & Majluf, N. S. (1984). Corporate financing and investment decisions when firms have information that investors do not have. *Journal of Financial Economics, 13*(2), 187–221.
Ortiz-Molina, H., & Penas, M. F. (2008). Lending to small businesses: The role of loan maturity in addressing information problems. *Small Business Economics, 30*(4), 361–383.
Schulze, W. S., & Kellermanns, F. W. (2015). Reifying socioemotional wealth. *Entrepreneurship Theory and Practice, 39*, 447–459.
Steijvers, T., & Voordeckers, W. (2016). Credit rationing in family firms: Short-term vs. long-term bank debt rationing. In *The Routledge Companion to Family Business* (pp. 205–224). New York: Routledge.
Yen, J. F., Lin, C. Y., Chen, Y. S., & Huang, Y. C. (2015). Founding family firms and bank loan contracts. *Journal of Financial Services Research, 48*(1), 53–82.

MIX
Papier aus verantwortungsvollen Quellen
Paper from responsible sources
FSC® C105338
FSC
www.fsc.org

If you have any concerns about our products,
you can contact us on
ProductSafety@springernature.com

In case Publisher is established outside the EU,
the EU authorized representative is:
Springer Nature Customer Service Center GmbH
Europaplatz 3, 69115 Heidelberg, Germany

Printed by Libri Plureos GmbH
in Hamburg, Germany